EVIL KNITS

20 Projects that go Bump in the Night

HANNAH SIMPSON

BLOOMSBURY

A QUINTET BOOK

© 2012 Quintet Publishing

First published in 2012 by Bloomsbury Publishing Plc by arrangement with
Quintet Publishing.
Bloomsbury Publishing Plc
50 Bedford Square
London WC1B 3DP

This book was conceived, designed and produced by
Quintet Publishing Limited
6 Blundell Street
London N7 9BH

QTT.EVK

Project Editor: Lindsay Kaubi
Designers: Jane Laurie, Zoë White, A+E Creative
Illustrator: Jane Laurie
Photographer: Marianne Paraskeva
Art Director: Michael Charles
Editorial Director: Donna Gregory
Publisher: Mark Searle

ISBN: 978-1-4081-4706-1

Manufactured in China

2 4 6 8 10 9 7 5 3 1

CONTENTS

Foreword

Hello and welcome to my collection of evil knitting patterns! If you're looking for something out of the ordinary, or a project with a twist, you've come to the right place. The horror genre is an endless source of inspiration for me and I've included only a few of the many things I find disturbing, creepy or cool. Toy and figure knitting is my first love, but here you will also find useful artifacts as well as some weird and wonderful decorations and curios. Not to mention zombies, of course!

This book assumes a basic level of knitting skill, but there are still patterns for every level of ability. If you've never worked with electronics or soft circuits, my easy-peasy LED Light-up Ghost is a great place to start. Once you've learned how to make a soft circuit switch, you'll think of a hundred cool ways to use them! Some of the projects require more construction than your typical knitting project – the Haunted House and the Monster Merry-Go-Round for example – but the results are worth it!

I hope you'll be inspired by this collection of fun things to knit. Most, if not all, of the projects are endlessly customizable. Unless tension is specifically mentioned, there's no need to worry about knitting swatches before you start (hooray!). Feel free to experiment with different colours and textures – it's what makes knitting so much fun, after all. If you are new to knitting, take a look at the stitch abbreviations on page 126 before you get started.

Hannah

Materials and Equipment

On the following pages you'll find information on all the tools and equipment you'll need to make the projects in this book. From essentials such as knitting needles to equipment for more advanced techniques.

Knitting needles

Modern needles are usually made of lightweight metal, wood, bamboo or plastic and are supplied in a full range of sizes, both in diameter and length. In most cases, the size is marked either on the side of the needle or on the 'stopper' at the end. The size of the needles required for any project is determined by the thickness of the yarn and the number of stitches the project requires.

The choice of material is mainly down to personal preference. However, some materials will be particularly suited to certain yarns, fibres or projects. For example, steel and aluminium needles are slippery and therefore good for fluffy or 'sticky' yarns such as mohair, while bamboo needles are slightly 'grippier' so are better for slippery yarns like silk. Double-pointed needles are sets of four or five needles, pointed at both ends.

Needle sizes

The US uses its own system for differentiating needle size (US size). Otherwise, knitting needle size is given in millimeters (mm) in Europe, and measures the diameter of the shaft of the needle; therefore, the larger the number, the thicker the needle. International knitting magazines and books should give needle sizes in both mm and in US size. You will need all the knitting needles stated in the pattern if you knit to the tension the designer has given. Edges and hems are generally knitted on a smaller needle, and long edges may require a circular needle to fit all the stitches.

Circular needles

Circular knitting needles are two short needles joined together by a cord. They (like double-pointed needles) allow you to knit 'in the round' to produce tubular knitting such as socks. When working in the round, you need to work only knit or plain rows because your work is not turned at the end of each row. However, circular needles can also be used in the same way as a pair of traditional needles by working knit and purl rows and turning the work at the end of each row. They are especially useful in this case when you are working wide projects with lots of stitches, such as blankets.

Needle gauge and ruler

A needle gauge with a ruler is useful if you own knitting needles without size markings, or are converting sizes from metric to US or vice versa. Simply slide a needle through successive holes until you find the correct size. The printing by the side of the hole that fits your needle tells you the needle size. One side has a ruler, while the other side shows the needle gauge.

Row counters

Row counters are used to help you count the number of rows you have worked. They are particularly useful when working complicated lace or cable patterns.

Cable needles

Made from metal, plastic or wood, cable needles are used when knitting cables to temporarily hold stitches. They can be straight, have a bend in the middle or be U-shaped.

Straight needles come in many materials and sizes.

The cords of circular needles come in varying lengths for work in the round of differing circumference.

Row counter: turn the dial to count rows worked.

Double-pointed needles are pointed at both ends for working in the round.

Cable needles are used for creating the twists in Aran knitting.

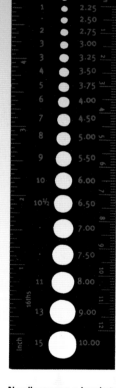

Needle gauge: a handy tool for any needle kit to help decipher needle size and to measure tension.

Other Equipment

People who knit regularly end up acquiring a range of tools and equipment designed to make the process easier and more accurate. The pages that follow take you through the basics you will encounter on knitting websites and in stores. There are many more items available and you will end up personalizing your own kit, but these are the essentials.

Scissors and tape measure

A pair of small, sharp scissors is an essential tool for trimming loose yarn ends. As you make a knitted project, you will often be required to take measurements. It is a good idea to have a tape measure that has inches and centimeters clearly marked on the same side.

Stitch holders

You will find these particularly useful where stitches need to be left unworked in order to work later on. Stitches can unravel easily when slipped off a knitting needle so a safety pin or stitch holder is helpful for keeping stitches from dropping. The stitches slip from the knitting needle onto the holder in the same way as you would slip a stitch from one needle to another (see page 16).

Point protectors

These protect the points of your knitting needles and keep your knitting from slipping off the needles when you are not working on it.

Pins and needles

Choose pins with brightly coloured tips, as they are much easier to see. The most common pins found in stores are the plastic-headed straight pins most commonly used for dressmaking – these are fine if you need to pin only a small area. It is also possible to buy specific

knitters' pins that are longer and thicker and have large, flat heads – these tend to be more stable than sewing pins.

Knitters' sewing or tapestry needles come in various sizes. The eye needs to be large enough to accommodate the knitting yarn and the point should be relatively blunt.

Stitch markers

Stitch markers are used as an alternative to knitters' pins and are useful for counting stitches and pattern repeats (see page 9) as well as marking the beginning of a round in circular knitting. They can be slipped through a knitted stitch and caught on the yarn, or placed over the knitting needle when beginning a large cast-on or working in the round.

Yarn bobbins

When using different colours in a Fair Isle or intarsia design, you may find it easier to wind small amounts of yarn around a bobbin instead of working directly from the ball, to prevent tangling.

Crochet hooks

Crochet hooks can be used to join knitted pieces and to create decorative edgings.

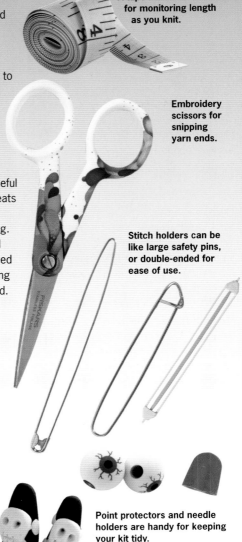

A tape measure is essential for monitoring length as you knit.

Embroidery scissors for snipping yarn ends.

Stitch holders can be like large safety pins, or double-ended for ease of use.

Point protectors and needle holders are handy for keeping your kit tidy.

Use pins with big heads so they do not disappear through the knitting.

Darning needle: a blunt needle prevents the yarn splitting when sewing up.

A crochet hook is a handy tool for picking up stitches.

Stitch markers can be open, closed or lockable to mark rows, stitching or important places in your work.

Notes on tension

When knitting toys and other non-wearables, knitting a tension swatch is often not necessary, providing you still use the same sized needles and yarn weight as the pattern dictates. If the pattern states that a tension swatch is required, you should make one to ensure your project turns out the correct size and shape. In these cases, the pattern will list the number of stitches and rows to 10cm (4in). If you find you have more stitches and rows to 10cm (4in), use a larger knitting needle. If you have worked fewer stitches and rows, use a smaller needle to achieve the correct tension.

The diameter of the knitting needle affects the size of the stitch, so stitches knitted on a chunky needle will take up more space than those knitted on a fine one. Also, be aware that your own personal tension is linked to technique and can change with practice. It can even be dependent on your mood or the situation in which you are knitting!

If you have knitted too tightly or too loosely, then your finished project will be the wrong size. Not only that, but the amount of yarn that you need to complete the project will change.

Making a tension swatch and measuring tension

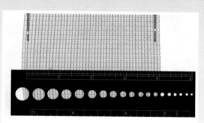

Step 1 Knit a small square of just over 10 x 10cm (4 x 4in) in the main yarn and stitch used in the pattern. Lay your knitted tension swatch flat.

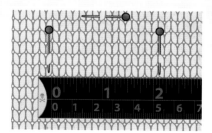

Step 2 Using a ruler (or tape measure), measure across a horizontal row of stitches and place a marker pin at the 10cm (4in) point. Do the same for the vertical rows of stitches.

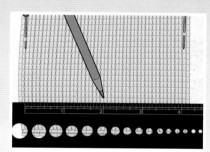

Step 3 Use the point of a knitting needle or pencil to count the number of stitches and rows between each pin.

Knitting Know-how

The basic techniques on these pages will get you started if you've never knitted before and are a great refresher for the more experienced.

Holding the needles

There is no absolutely correct way to hold your needles but there are two more common methods: like a pen or like a knife. You may find that both hands want to hold the needles in the same way, but if it is comfortable, you can hold each needle in a different way. There are also some variations on how needles are held in different countries.

Knife hold

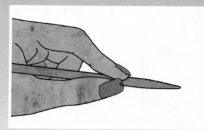

Pen hold

English method
The left hand takes the weight of the needles while the stitch is being made. The yarn is held in the right hand and wraps around the right needle.

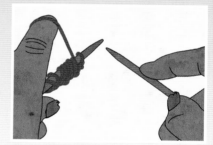

Continental method
The yarn is held in the left hand and the right needle 'picks' the yarn from the left hand.

Making a slip knot

A knitted fabric is made by working rows of stitches in various sequences. In order to create a fabric, you must first make a base row, known as a cast-on row. A slip knot is used as the first stitch for a cast-on row.

Step 1 Holding the yarn in both hands, make a small loop in the yarn. Take the piece that you are holding in the right hand underneath the loop.

Step 2 Pull this piece of yarn through the original loop to create a knot and place the slip knot onto the knitting needle.

Casting on

Casting on is the first step in knitting and it provides the first row of loops on the needle. Different methods of casting on produce different edges, each with its own use. It is a good idea to practise all of these variations at some stage. If a pattern does not state which cast on to use, simply use your favourite method.

The thumb method

This method is perfect for creating a stretchy edge for an edge where elasticity is required, such as a ribbed cuff. You cannot use it in the middle of the work – try the two-needle or cable method. If you are a continental knitter, you will not be able to work this cast on; try the continental method instead for an alternative.

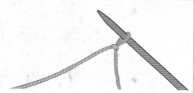

Step 1 Make a slip knot in your yarn, leaving a long tail of approximately three times the length of the desired width of your fabric. Place the slip knot onto the needle and hold needle in your right hand.

Step 3 With the left thumb upright, slip right-hand needle through the loop made around the thumb from bottom to top.

Step 5 Draw the loop just made around the needle through the loop on the thumb.

Step 2 Grab the long tail loose end of the yarn in your left hand and make a loop around your left thumb with this end, still holding tight to the loose end.

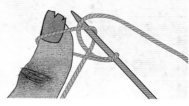

Step 4 Wrap ball end of yarn around right-hand needle as if knitting normally.

Step 6 This is the resulting cast on stitch alongside the slip knot. Now repeat steps 2–5 for desired amount of stitches.

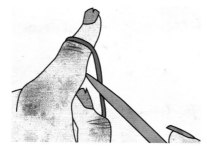

Backward loop cast on

If using this technique to cast on, start with a slip knot, but when using this cast on to add stitches in the middle of a row, there's no need to make a slip knot to begin.

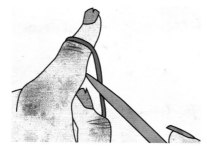

Step 1 Holding needle in one hand and yarn in the other hand, loop the working yarn and slip it onto the needle backwards so that it doesn't unwind.

Step 2 Gently pull taut and repeat.

Knit and purl stitches

Most knitting is based on combinations of just two basic stitches – knit stitch and purl stitch. Once you have mastered these two stitches, you can work many different stitch patterns.

Begin by casting on about 25–30 stitches using one of the methods on page 11.

Knit stitch

With knitting, the aim is to hold the needle with the stitches in your left hand, and transfer them all to the right needle by knitting another row. The knit stitch is the simplest of all stitches. Knitting every row forms the ridged fabric called garter stitch. Practise knit stitch until you can work it fairly smoothly, then practise purl stitch.

Purl stitch

Purl is the second basic knitting stitch. When you use purl in a fabric, you never work every row purl because this fabric would look exactly the same as garter stitch, and as the purl stitch is slightly more difficult, this is pointless. You usually work a row of purls followed by a row of knits, then alternate knit and purl every row. This is called stocking stitch.

Knit stitch

Step 1 Hold the needle with the stitches to be knitted in the left hand with the yarn behind the work.

Step 2 Insert the right-hand needle into a stitch from front to back. Take the yarn over it, forming a loop.

Step 3 Bring the needle and the new loop to the front of the work through the stitch and slide the original stitch off the left-hand needle.

Purl stitch

Step 1 Hold the stitches to be purled in the left hand, with the yarn at the front of the work.

Step 2 Insert the right-hand needle through the front of the stitch, from right to left. Take the yarn over and under, forming a loop.

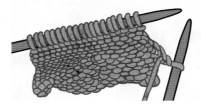

Step 3 Take the needle and the new loop through the back and slide the stitch off the left-hand needle.

Casting off

There is one simple and commonly used method of securing stitches once you have finished a piece of knitting: casting off. There are various methods of achieving this, a couple of examples of which are shown here. These captions show casting off along a knit row. However, you can cast off in pattern along any fabric, simply working each stitch as set in pattern, instead of knitting all stitches across the row.

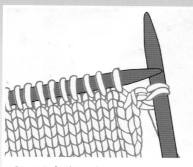

Step 1 At the point where you are ready to cast off, knit the first two stitches.

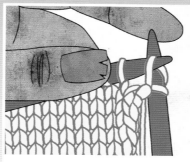

Step 2 Slip the left-hand needle into the first stitch on the right-hand needle, and lift it over the second stitch and off the needle.

Sewn cast off

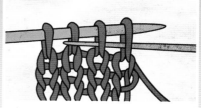

Step 1 Cut the working yarn, leaving a tail three times the length of the item you are casting off. Thread your yarn into a yarn needle. Working right to left, insert the sewing needle into the first two stitches as if to purl and pull the yarn through.

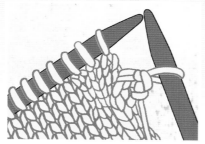

Step 3 Knit the next stitch so that there are two stitches on the right-hand needle again.

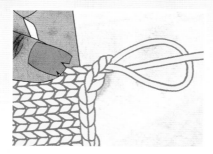

Step 4 Repeat steps 2 and 3 until all stitches are knitted from the left-hand needle and one stitch remains on the right-hand needle. Make the last stitch loop larger, break the yarn and draw it firmly through the last stitch to fasten off.

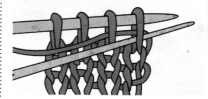

Step 2 Reinsert the needle into the first stitch on the knitting needle as if to knit, pull the yarn through and slip the stitch off the needle. Repeat.

Basic stitch variations

All knitting, however complicated, is made up of combinations of just two stitches: knit and purl. Combining these two stitches is the key to a world of variation in your knitting.

Garter stitch

If you were to work rows of just knit, or rows of just purl stitches in succession, you would create a knitted fabric known as garter stitch. This is quite textural and sturdy and looks the same on both sides of the fabric.

Garter stitch looks the same on both sides.

Stocking stitch

Stocking stitch fabric is different on both sides and therefore has a right side, or front, and a wrong side, or back. The sides of the fabric are also respectively referred to as a knit side and a purl side.

The right side is smooth, and you will be able to see that the stitches create a zigzag effect. The wrong side is bumpy and looks a little like garter stitch.

To make a fabric using stocking stitch, work rows of knit stitches and rows of purl stitches alternately. If you have the smooth side of the fabric facing you as you begin the row, you will need to work a knit row in order to keep the pattern correct. If you have the more textural side facing you at the beginning of the row, you will need to work a purl row.

Stocking stitch: front or right side.

Reverse stocking stitch: back or wrong side.

Ribbing

A knit rib is simply a mix of knits and purls across a row. A rib can be any mix of knits and purls built up on top of each other in vertical lines or 'ribs'. A ribbed fabric is very stretchy and is therefore great in areas such as cuffs, where the fabric needs to grip more tightly to the body.

Ribbing is great when stretch is needed, such as for socks or cuffs.

Working knit and purl stitches in the same row

If you want to create textural patterns, you will need to work both knit and purl stitches in the same row. It is important that you change from a knit to a purl stitch and vice versa in the correct way.

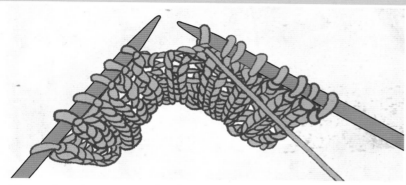

Changing from a purl stitch to a knit stitch

Having completed a purl stitch, the yarn will be held at the front of the work. In order to work a subsequent knit stitch, take the yarn to the back of the work between both knitting needles. Then knit the next stitch.

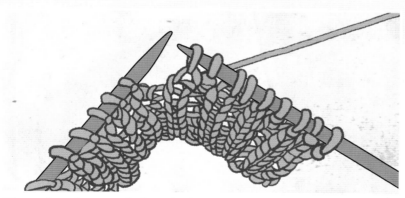

Changing from a knit stitch to a purl stitch

Having completed a knit stitch, the yarn will be held at the reverse of the work. In order to work a subsequent purl stitch, bring the yarn through to the front of the work between both knitting needles, then purl the next stitch.

Fur stitch

This stitch, which is used in one of the projects in this book, is a fabulous pile fabric that can be left loopy or cut to create a rug effect. (For stitch abbreviations see page 126.)

Cast on any multiple of sts and work a fur stitch row on an RS row as often as you wish depending on desired pile. Work all non-fur rows as a k row.

Fur stitch row (RS): K next st without letting it drop off the LH needle, yfwd, pass yarn around thumb or piece of cardboard to make loop approx 2cm (1in) long (or desired length), yb and k into the back of st on LH needle, this time completing it by letting it drop off. Pass 1st loop of the st (now on RH needle) over 2nd loop of st and off the needle to secure st.

Shaping

To shape a knitted piece, you have to increase and decrease stitches. There are different ways of doing this and most knitters have their own preferences. Decreasing and increasing are also used to create a variety of stitches such as bobbles and lace patterns.

Patterns will often use different methods of increasing and decreasing for different parts of a pattern, due to the way in which differing stitches lie within the increase/decrease. For example, when shaping a raglan sleeve, it is preferable that the stitches lie in the direction of the shaping. Stitches on the right side of the raglan shaping need to form a slope that points to the left and stitches on the left side need to create a slope that points to the right. When these shapings are used as a feature, this is known as 'fully fashioning'.

Decreasing

You may be required to decrease stitches by working two or more stitches together in techniques such as lacework and when shaping a knitted piece.

There are many ways to do this and the most common and simplest way is to knit or purl two or more stitches together as in the following instructions.

Slipping a stitch

In order to create some textural fabrics such as lace, or when shaping a piece of knitting, you may be required to slip stitches from one needle to another, without knitting them.

To slip a stitch knitwise

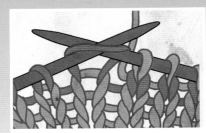

Slide the right-hand needle through the next stitch on the left needle from front to back, as if to knit. Let the stitch drop from the left needle and pass it onto the right knitting needle without knitting.

To slip a stitch purlwise

Slide the right-hand needle through the next stitch on the left needle from right to left as if to purl. Let the stitch drop from the left needle and pass it onto the right needle without knitting.

K2tog

Decreasing is most commonly done by working two or more stitches together to form one stitch. On a knit, or right-side, row this creates a slope to the right.

Step 1 Slide the right needle through the second and then the first stitches on the left needle from front to back. Wrap the yarn around the right needle as a normal knit stitch.

Step 2 Knit the two stitches together as if knitting normally and slide both from the left needle.

P2tog

Working two or more stitches together on the wrong side of the knitted piece creates a slope to the right on the right side.

Step 1 Slide the right needle through the first two stitches on the left needle 'purlwise'.

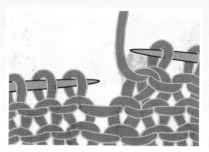

Step 2 Purl the two stitches together as if purling normally and slide both from the left needle.

S1, K1, PSSO/SKPO

The slip one, knit one, pass slipped stitch over technique is probably the easiest of left-leaning decreasing techniques and is also abbreviated as skpo for brevity.

Step 1 Slip the first stitch by placing the right needle through it as if knitting, and slide it from the left needle. Knit the next stitch.

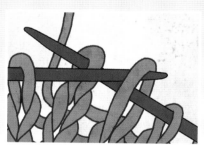

Step 2 Using the left needle, pass the slipped stitch on the right needle over the top of the knitted stitch.

SSK

This is simply slipping the next two stitches, then knitting them together – it is very similar to working a k2tog tbl but some find it easier to achieve.

Step 1 Slip next two sts knitwise onto right-hand needle.

Step 2 Insert left-hand needle into front of both sts from left to right.

Step 3 Knit both sts tog.

Increasing

There are many ways to increase, and increasing is usually done on the right side of the work. Patterns do not always specify how to increase and may just give the instruction to 'make' or increase a number of stitches: m1 or inc.

Inc

This usually means knitting into the front and then the back of a stitch. This increase is best worked at either the beginning or end of the knitted piece, as it is not very neat.

Step 1 Work to where the extra stitch is needed. Knit into the front of the next stitch on the left knitting needle without slipping it off.

Step 2 With the stitch still on the left needle and the yarn at the back, knit into the back of the same stitch and slip it from the needle.

M1

This is a neat increase, usually done by knitting into the back of the bar between stitches.

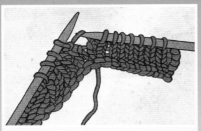

Step 1 Pass the right knitting needle underneath the 'bar' of yarn between two stitches from front to back.

Step 2 Slip the loop onto the left needle and remove the right needle.

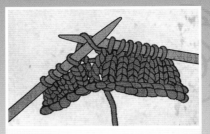

Step 3 Knit into the back of the loop to twist it, by inserting the right needle behind the yarn on the left needle from right to left.

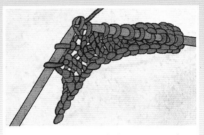

Step 4 Finish the stitch as a normal knit stitch, remove the left needle, pass the new stitch onto the right needle.

Short row shaping/ increasing by casting on

This is a form of shaping that creates flowing, neat curves and 3-D shapes within your flat knitting and can be achieved very easily. At their most basic, short rows are part-finished rows, creating stitches in parts of your knitting that are worked more frequently or for more rows than other stitches, meaning you're adding shaped rows into your work without adding or casting on extra stitches – you always have the same amount of stitches on the needle.

Short rows can be worked at the shoulder to create a more elegant finish without obvious 'steps'. They are perfect for sock heels, darts and for making shawl collars.

A short row is created by working across to the allocated turn mark (or knitting the correct amount of stitches), then turning the work and leaving the remaining stitches in the row unworked.

When you work a short row into the knit piece, you must make a smooth transition between the sides of the work with varying amounts of rows. Do this by wrapping a slipped stitch as follows. Work to turn point, slip next stitch purlwise onto right needle. Bring yarn to front. Slip same stitch back to left needle unworked. Turn work and bring yarn into correct position for next stitch, wrapping the stitch as you do so.

Sometimes these wrapped stitches are visible, so if you wish you can hide them as follows.

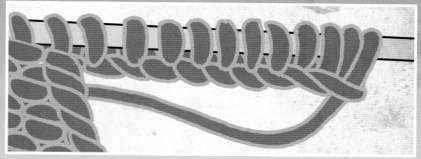

Increasing by casting on

At the end of a row, if you need to increase a lot of stitches, you can simply cast them on.

Knit stitch: On right side, work to just before wrapped stitch. Insert right needle from front, under the wrap from bottom up and then into wrapped stitch as usual. Knit them together, making sure new stitch comes out under wrap.

Purl stitch: On wrong side, work to just before wrapped stitch. Insert right needle from back, under wrap from bottom up and put on left needle. Purl them together.

Weaving in ends

Never cut the loose ends of yarn left at the edges of your knitting to any less than 10–20cm (4–8in) long, as these can slip through the loops of the stitches easily and unravel. However, these ends do need to be tidied.

There are many ways of doing this by threading the ends in and out of the stitches on the reverse side of the work in any way that makes the length become invisible. This can be achieved by hooking the yarn through with a small crochet hook, or weaving in and out using a large tapestry needle. This needle needs to be blunt in order to ensure the point only passes through the stitches and not the actual yarn, which can become messy.

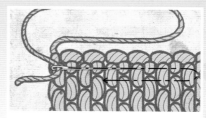

Step 1 Thread the yarn through the loops along the edge of the work for around 4–5cm (1½–2in), then sew back through a few of the last loops to secure.

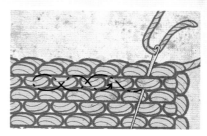

Step 2 Pass the end through the stitches, inserting the needle from the top of the loop on the first, then the bottom on the next alternately for about 4–5cm (1½–2in), then sew back through a few of the last loops to secure.

Finishing Techniques

Bad finishing can be really noticeable in seams; therefore, a mattress stitch, sewn with a blunt tapestry needle, is the best way to make them. In a stocking stitch or ribbed fabric this is invisible if properly done.

Seaming

With right sides of both pieces of fabric towards you, secure yarn at the bottom of one piece. Pass the needle to the other section and pick up one stitch, which you can see on the needle in the picture below. Pull the yarn through and pull tightly. Insert the needle through one stitch of the first section, entering where the yarn exited previously. Continue in this way, from one side to the other, as if lacing a corset, until you reach the last stitch. Secure tightly. If you have entered through the right section, the seam will be virtually indistinguishable from the rest of the fabric.

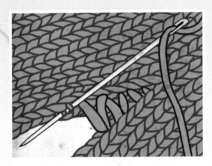

Always use the same colour yarn as in the main body of work (here, the colour is contrasting in order to highlight the technique) so that when the seams are pulled and moved when worn, the joining yarn cannot be seen. Some yarns may be too weak or fancy to sew along a seam, so double these up, add a stronger yarn to the original, or use a different yarn, but in the same colour.

Grafting

Grafting the toe in a sock is the original use for this technique, but it works very well for many different seams: any two pieces of knitting that have been left on the needles rather than bound off can be grafted together using 'Kitchener stitch' or grafting for an invisible seam.

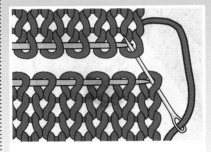

Step 1 Using the knitting yarn, work from right to left. From the back of the fabric, bring the needle through the first knitted stitch of the lower fabric and through the first stitch of the upper fabric.

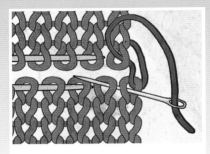

Step 2 From the front, thread the needle back through the centre of the first stitch on the lower fabric where the yarn leaves, then out of the centre of the next stitch on the left.

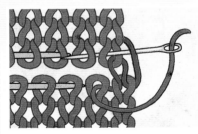

Step 3 Thread the needle through the centre of the top stitch and along the centre of the next. Continue like this and, as each stitch is worked, keep slipping the knitting needle from them.

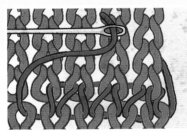

Step 4 Continue like this. To finish, pull the yarn tight, cut it off and weave in yarn ends on the inside of the work.

Vertical buttonhole

Buttonholes can be worked by casting off a certain number of stitches on one row, then casting them on again in the next.

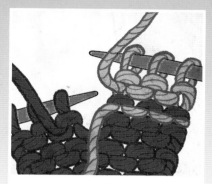

Step 1 Knit to the buttonhole position, turn and leave remaining stitches unworked on either a holder or on the needle. Work on these stitches for the desired length of buttonhole, then leave stitches on holder and rejoin yarn to unworked stitches on first holder.

Step 2 Work these stitches until the same length of fabric has been worked as for the first side of the buttonhole. Work 1 row across these stitches and those left on second holder to complete the buttonhole.

Blocking

It is amazing how much can be achieved to neaten your finished knitted pieces with simple blocking techniques.

Blocking must always be done prior to sewing the pieces up, to ensure all are the same size and do not become misshapen once sewn together. Basic garment pieces can sometimes be simply pinned into shape and then lightly steamed with an iron set to 'full steam' to set the stitches, but a word of warning: do not press with the iron, this will flatten the fabric; simply hover it over the surface and allow the steam to work its magic.

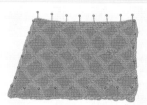

Step 1 Lay each piece down, with the right side facing, onto a clean, very slightly damp towel and pin into shape. If you wish to ensure that two identical pieces are the exact same size and shape, pin them on top of each other as a guide.

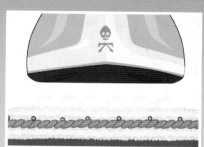

Step 2 Lay another damp towel over the top and lightly pass over with an iron, without pressing, but with the 'full steam' option selected. You must let the steam and moisture do the work, rather than the weight of the iron, as this will flatten the stitches.

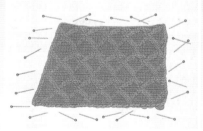

Step 3 Once the whole piece is warmed and steamed thoroughly, let it cool down and dry completely, then you can unpin and remove the pieces.

Circular Knitting and Intarsia

When working three-dimensional or unusual shapes, circular knitting can be extremely useful and is a technique used in many of the projects in this book. Intarsia is a great way of adding colour to your work and is planned out on coloured charts.

When working stocking stitch in the round, you never need to purl – you can just knit every row without turning, as you are effectively always on the same side of the knitting. However, this means that to do garter stitch (usually knit every row), you will need to alternate between knit and purl rows. There are many advantages to working with sets of four double-pointed needles or a pair of circular needles, and they are especially useful when using the Fair Isle technique or working neckbands or cuffs. The only technique that cannot be worked in the round is intarsia. As with all knitting, work a swatch to judge the tension, as this can change when you are using a combination of knit and purl rows. However, do remember if you are working stocking stitch that the tension will be different from usual, as you will never have to do a purl row when working in the round – usually this purl row can differ greatly in tension. Therefore, you need to do your tension swatch in the round, too.

Circular needles

Make sure the circular needle you choose is long enough to hold the number of stitches in the pattern. However, remember that if the length of needle is too long, the stitches won't stretch all the way around the cord to complete a round unless you use the magic loop. Cast on the stitches and spread them along the length of the circular needle, making sure that the row is not twisted. Mark the first stitch with a contrast thread or stitch marker to keep track of the beginning of the round.

Double-pointed needles

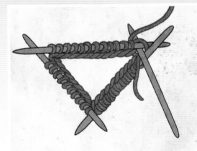

Double-pointed needles, or dpns, are available in sets of four or five. Divide the stitches evenly between three or four of the needles and, once the cast-on row has been made, use the fourth/fifth needle to knit. Once all the stitches from one needle have been knitted onto the fourth, use the free needle to work the stitches from the next needle. Keep the tension of the stitches constant when transferring from one needle to another; always draw the yarn up firmly when knitting the first stitch at the changeover point to avoid a ladder or loopy stitch. As with circular needles, ensure the cast-on row is not twisted before you start knitting and use a stitch marker to identify the first stitch.

The magic loop

This technique can be used on smallish sets of stitches if you find double-pointed needles daunting, or if you want to use just one needle all the way up a project that decreases in stitches, such as a hat.

You will need a very long needle – at least 80cm (30in), but preferably 1m (39in) circular or longer if possible.

Cast on the stitches and divide them in half equally, placing half on one needle and the rest on the cord. Pull a length of the cord through the gap between the two sets of stitches. Make sure that the row is not twisted. Join for working in the round by placing a marker for the first stitch of the round, then pull the right-

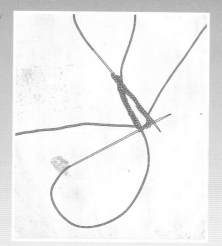

Intarsia

Bobbins

Bobbins are used when you do not wish to have a whole ball of yarn attached to the knitted piece while working intarsia. Bobbins can be bought ready-made with the yarn wrapped around them, or you can make your own. For larger areas of colour you may wish to wrap the yarn in small plastic bags, secured with rubber bands.

To make your own bobbin

hand needle slightly out of its stitches, while leaving the other half of the stitches on the left-hand needle. Knit the stitches from the left-hand needle normally, using the right-hand needle, pulling tightly on the yarn for the first couple of stitches to ensure the round joins seamlessly.

The right-hand needle will now have stitches on it, and the left-hand needle will not. Therefore, you need to pull the cord so that the stitches on it are on the left-hand needle and then pull out the right-hand needle, leaving its stitches on the cord, so you can use it to knit off the left-hand needle. Continue in this way for the required length of fabric.

The intarsia method creates separate areas of colour within the knitted piece. A separate length of yarn is used for each section of coloured knitting and the yarns are twisted where they meet to create a single piece.

Intarsia is best worked over stocking stitch, although areas of more textural stitching, such as garter stitch and moss stitch, can also look very effective when used in conjunction with intarsia.

Before you settle down to work, read through the pattern carefully and check how much yarn you need in each colour. To work intarsia effectively you will need to learn a few basic techniques: bobbin winding, joining in new colours, and changing from one colour to another on both a knit and a purl row.

Step 1 Wrap the yarn around the thumb and finger of your right hand in the form of a figure of eight.

Step 2 Carefully remove the yarn from your fingers and cut it from the ball. Wind the loose end of yarn around the centre of the figure of eight and secure it tightly.

When using a bobbin, pull the yarn from the centre a little at a time and keep it as close to the work as possible to avoid tangling.

Joining in a new colour

You may find that a new colour of yarn is needed across a row of stitches, or that an existing bobbin is running out. In these cases you will need to join in a new colour.

Step 1 Insert the right-hand needle into the next stitch. Place the yarn over the working yarn and between the two needles, with the tail end to the left side.

Step 2 Bring the new yarn up from under the existing yarn and knit, dropping both yarns from the left-hand needle after you have done so.

Changing colours

When working an intarsia design, coloured areas of stitching are worked from separate balls (or bobbins). If these areas are not joined together in some way, you will end up with individual pieces of colour with large gaps in between. Simply cross the yarns to ensure that the knitting stays as one piece.

Changing colour on a knit row:

Work to the point where you need to change colour. Insert the right-hand needle into the next stitch knitwise. Take the first colour over the top of the second colour and drop. Pick up the second colour, ensuring that the yarns remain twisted, and continue according to the pattern.

Changing colour on a purl row:

Work to the point where you need to change colour. Insert the right-hand needle into the next stitch purlwise. Take the first colour over the top of the second colour and drop. Pick up the second colour, ensuring that the yarns remain twisted, and continue the pattern.

Reading a graph

All intarsia and most Fair Isle patterns are set out in the form of a graph. Graphs are read from bottom to top; read from right to left on a knit row, and from left to right on a purl row (if you knit in rows). When knitting in the round, read graphs from bottom to top, from right to left on each row of the graph.

Most patterns are now printed in colour, but those printed in black and white will have a key to one side describing what colours are placed where, with each colour represented by a symbol.

It is a good idea to photocopy the pattern, so that you can mark off rows as you knit without ruining your master copy, or use a ruler to mark the row you are on. Photocopying is also useful if the graph is small, as you can enlarge it to a more readable size.

Each square on an intarsia chart represents a stitch and each horizontal row, a row of knitting.

Embellishments

The projects in this book are embellished using a wide range of methods. Demonstrated here are the knitted embellishments, including picot edgings and i-cord, as well as step-by-step instructions for the embroidery stitches used in the book and instructions on making pompoms.

Picot cast off

This is a pretty edging for a bound-off edge/neckline. Work on a multiple of 3 sts, plus 2, until you are ready to cast off.

Step 1 Cast off two stitches, one stitch on the right needle.

Step 2 *Slip this stitch back to the left-hand needle, cast on 2 sts, cast off 4 sts; rep from * to end of row. Fasten off yarn.

Crocheted picot edging

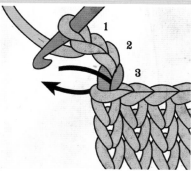

Step 1 Single crochet into the edge of the knitted fabric, then chain 3.

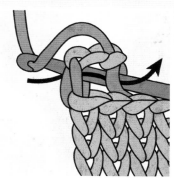

Step 2 Insert the hook into the third chain from the hook and slip stitch into it. Then single crochet into fabric again and repeat the picot edging technique as required.

I-cord

An I-cord is a quick and simple way to make a cord, or tube of knitting, using two double-pointed needles. Use the cord as a button loop, a drawstring or as an embellishment.

Cast on any amount of sts, but a small number will create the neatest, closed cord. Three to 5 stitches are perfect. Work quite tightly, with needles slightly smaller than suggested.

Step 1 Using two double-pointed needles, cast on set number of stitches and k 1 row.

Step 2 Instead of turning a row, slide stitches to opposite end of the needle, and passing yarn from left of work to right, knit another row to roll stitches into a tube. Continue in this way for every foll row. Fasten off yarn.

Embroidery

Simple embroidery stitches can be used to add details, features and interest to your knitting projects.

Running stitch

Pass the needle in and out of the fabric, making the stitches of equal lengths. The stitches on the underside should also be of equal length, but half the size or less than the upper stitches.

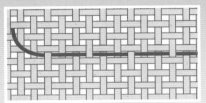

French knot

Bring the needle through where required and wrap the thread twice around the needle. Holding the thread taut, insert the needle back into the work as close as possible (but not in the exact same spot) to where it emerged. Pull through gently, holding the thread down until it's all pulled through.

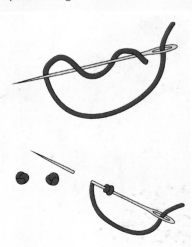

Chain stitch

Bring the needle through from the back. In one motion, take the yarn through from front to back at the point where the first yarn came through to the front to create a loop of yarn on the right side. Bring the needle back through to the front, a short distance along the line of your design and through the centre of the loop. Tighten and repeat. At the end of the line, hold down the last loop with a small stitch over the loop.

Blanket stitch

Working from left to right, bring the needle through the piece from the back, a short distance in from the edge of the fabric. From the front, thread the needle through to the back, a short space to the right, with the tip inside the loop of thread, and pull through.

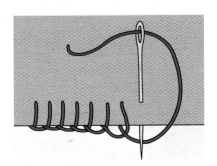

Duplicate stitch

Duplicate stitch copies the structure and appearance of a knitted stitch.

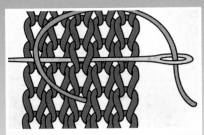

Step 1 Bring the needle out at the base of the knitted stitch to be duplicated. Pass the needle behind the two 'legs' of the stitch above and pull through.

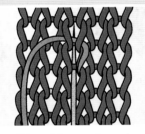

Step 2 Insert the needle again at the base of the same knitted stitch where it first emerged and bring it out at the base of the next knitted stitch to be duplicated.

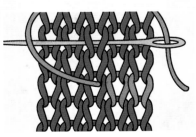

Step 3 Repeat as needed.

Making a pompom

Step 1 First, decide what size you want your pompom to be, draw two outer circles on your card about 10 per cent larger than the diameter that you want – the extra 10 per cent allows for trimming and tidying. Draw two smaller circles inside the first two circles about half the diameter of the finished pompom size.

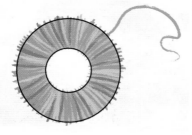

Step 2 Cut out the doughnut shapes from the card and, holding them together, begin winding your yarn around the doughnut. Start inside the hole and wind around the card and back through the centre. Continue until the centre hole is filled in, using a needle for the last few wraps.

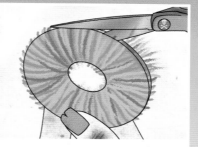

Step 3 Use a pair of scissors and, cutting a few strands at a time, cut between the two doughnuts of card.

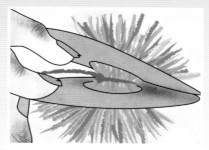

Step 4 Pry the two pieces of card apart and tie a length of yarn tightly around the centre of the pompom. Remove the card and trim your pompom as desired.

Soft Circuits

Don't be scared by the electronics involved in making soft circuits – it's easy, even for beginners. You don't need to worry about getting an electric shock or blowing anything up. We're working with very low voltages here.

Sewing with LEDs

LED stands for Light Emitting Diode. These are tiny little lights that run on very low voltages without getting hot. An LED has two wire 'legs' – one longer than the other. The longer leg is the positive – in order for your LED to light up, the positive leg of the LED must connect to the positive side of your battery.

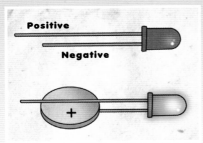

This is how the light is made to go inside the little Light-up Ghost (see page 76). The legs are then simply taped into position to keep the light on. The battery should last around 48 hours before it needs replacing.

Preparing the LED

To make an LED suitable for sewing into a circuit, you need to bend the legs into loops using needle-nose pliers. Before you do this, though, make a mark on the longer leg with a permanent marker or a dab of nail varnish. This will enable you to identify the positive leg when the legs are coiled up.

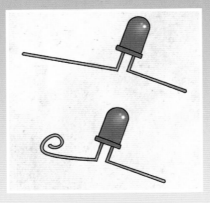

Making the circuit

Conductive thread contains metal and has the ability to conduct a small amount of voltage. This thread can be used in a soft circuit to extend the distance between the battery and the LED. The projects in this book use a felt patch to mount the soft circuit. The shape and dimensions of the patch depend on which project you are making.

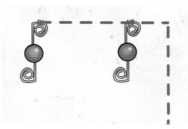

Step 1 To begin making the circuit, take one of your prepared LEDs and position it on the felt patch with the positive leg/coil towards the top of the patch.

Step 2 Thread a needle with a length of conductive thread and sew the positive coil firmly into place. With the thread still attached, sew a line of running stitches horizontally across to where the second positive LED leg will be. Holding the LED in place, sew the other loop to the felt. Continue to sew a line of stitches down the side of the patch, towards where your switch will be.

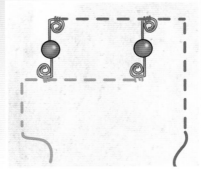

Step 3 With a new length of conductive thread, sew across the negative leg/coil in the same way. It's really important that your positive and negative threads don't touch at any point – this will cause a short circuit and your LEDs won't light up.

Making a pressure switch

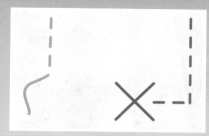

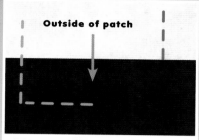

Outside of patch

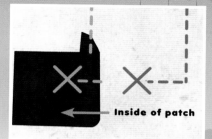

Inside of patch

Apart from the LED Light-up Ghost, all the electronic projects in this book use a pressure switch. This makes an electrical connection when pressed, which lights up the LED. Without a switch, battery life is reduced considerably. Your pressure switch will be mounted on the same patch as the LEDs. The instructions below assume that you have already sewn your LEDs in place, as described on page 28.

Step 1 First, locate where on the patch you want your battery to be. Re-thread your needle with the positive thread that is attached to the tops of your LEDs and sew a horizontal line leading to a large X. The X should be about the same size as your battery.

Step 2 Now, cut a smaller felt patch – the size of this depends on the project you're making and will be detailed in the instructions. Thread your needle with the negative thread, then, holding the patch in place so that it matches up widthways with the main patch, sew through both pieces. First sew down, then across; finally, stitch another big X on the underside of the patch to match up with the positive X. The two Xs should be touching.

At this stage, if you place a battery between the two felt pieces, with the positive side of the battery matching the positive X, the LEDs will light up.

Step 3 To make the switch work properly, cut two more pieces of felt measuring 2 x 2cm (¾ x ¾in). Cut a hole in the centre of each of these pieces by folding them in half and snipping a square out of the middle to make a square doughnut shape. Then glue one piece over the negative X and one piece over the positive X.

Step 4
Finally, thread your needle with white thread and, with the battery correctly positioned, sew all around the edges of the patch to hold the battery in place. Using white thread makes it easier to unpick when the time comes to replace the battery. Your pressure switch is finished! Now, when you squeeze or press the felt where the battery is, the LEDs should light up. The soft circuit patch is now ready to use in your chosen project.

Project Selector

Whether you are looking for a unique gift to terrify a friend or relative, or just want to create something a little different, you're sure to find something in the sinister selection below.

Monkey with Miniature Cymbals
Pages 32–37
This tiny monkey will liven up anyone's desk with his mad, staring eyes.

Ferdy Hand Puppet
Pages 38–43
Terrorize your friends with this lifelike hand puppet, complete with felted finger knives.

Voodoo Doll Cat Toy
Pages 44–47
Let your cat take revenge on your enemies, while you put your feet up.

Necronomicon iPad Cosy
Pages 48–51
Summon horrors from another dimension! Or just check your email.

Shrunken Head in a Jar
Pages 52–55
Keep marauding cookie thieves at bay with this keeper of the cookie jar.

Zombie Egg Cosy
Pages 56–59
Grab your spoon and smash some zombie brains!

Freak Show Finger Puppets
Pages 60–65
Paying homage, in yarn, to history's finest sideshow performers.

Creepy Clown Cushion Cover
Pages 66–69
Add some carnival creepiness to your home with this intarsia cushion cover.

Monster Merry-Go-Round
Pages 70–75
This carousel is perfect for a baby. It's never too soon to introduce them to the dark side!

Light-up Ghost
Pages 76-79

These little ghosts are a great introduction to using electronics in your projects.

Abominable Snowman
Pages 80-85

Don't run away! Bigfoot's cold-weather cousin just wants you to give him a hug.

Kraken Tentacle
Pages 86-89

Every home needs a huge, cuddly, severed tentacle.

Nosferatu
Pages 90-95

The knitted version of this most sinister of vampires has glowing orange eyes.

Grue Wallet
Pages 96-99

Terrify your friends with this Grue Wallet. Perfect for the *Zork* fan in your life.

Zombie Marionette
Pages 100-105

Put on a show with your very own army of the undead.

Creature from the Black Lagoon Sleep Mask
Pages 106-109

Slip on this knitted sleep mask to enjoy some uninterrupted snoozing. After all, who would dare to disturb you?

Haunted House Diorama
Pages 110-123

Knit an entire haunted playhouse, with fold-down graveyard. Just what you've always wanted!

Pile O' Skulls

Why just want one skull when you can have a whole pile o' skulls?

Gravestones

Add a touch of classic horror chic to your knitted graveyard with these miniature gravestones.

Little Witches

Even the most hardened witch hunter would think twice before burning one of these cute little witches at the stake.

Haunted Tree

A twisted terror in tweed; perfect for your haunted house's garden.

Monkey with Miniature Cymbals

There's something undeniably creepy about old clockwork toys. Who's to say you won't wake to hear the faint chk chk chk of an ancient and rusty mechanism, working away in the dead of night. No such fears with this plush monkey, whose cymbals are made from yarn. All the better for sneaking up on you in the dark with!

This unsettling toy is featured in Stephen King's chilling short story, *The Monkey*, in which the seemingly harmless novelty is possessed by an evil spirit. The cymbal-playing chimp has come to signify approaching doom, as well as a slow descent into madness. Many cult-classic horror and science fiction films – from *Close Encounters of the Third Kind* to *The Devil's Gift*, *Phantom of the Opera* and even a popular modern video game, *Call of Duty,* showcase the disquieting wide-eyed monkey. It's even recognized worldwide, not least because the chimp's first incarnations came from a Japanese toy manufacturer in the 1950s. You'll find this fiendish primate in manga, anime and comics from across the globe… and soon, terrorizing your very own home.

The base of this manic monkey is weighted, so he will sit pleasingly on your desk at work – a welcome reminder that however monotonous your job gets, there's always someone worse off than you.

You will need:

- ☠ 3.5mm (size 4) double-pointed needles (dpns)
- ☠ 3mm (size 3) needles
- ☠ DK yarn in red, mid-brown, light brown/natural and yellow (Rowan Lurex Shimmer was used here)
- ☠ Polyester toy stuffing
- ☠ Dried split peas/lentils or polypropylene pellets (poly pellets) for weighting
- ☠ 2 x 12mm (⅜in) pink safety eyes
- ☠ Pipe cleaners
- ☠ Tapestry needle
- ☠ Thin card
- ☠ Pair of tights
- ☠ Compass and ruler

Body:

1. On 3.5mm (size 4) needles, cast on 4 stitches in red, for the base of the body. Increase to 8 by knitting into the front and back of each stitch (kfb). Divide between 3 needles and place marker.
2. Knit 1 round.
3. Kfb into every stitch (16 st).
4. Knit 1 round.
5. *K1, kfb* repeat around (24 st).
6. Knit 1 round.
7. *K2, kfb* repeat around (32 st).
8. Knit 1 round.
9. *K3, kfb* repeat around (40 st).
10. Knit 3 rounds.
11. *K8, k2tog* repeat around (36 st).
12. Knit 1 round.
13. *K7, k2tog* repeat around (32 st).
14. Knit 1 round.
15. *K6, k2tog* repeat around (28 st).
16. Knit 1 round.
17. *K5, k2tog* repeat around (24 st).
18. Knit 3 rounds.
19. Change to the mid-brown yarn and knit 10 rounds.
Leave on needles and weave in loose ends.

To weight the base of the monkey, cut the toe off a pair of old tights and fill with dried peas or poly pellets. Tie the top closed with a piece of yarn. Stuff this into the bottom of the body piece and fill the rest of the body with polyester stuffing up to the neck.

Head:

1. *K1, k2tog* repeat around (16 st).
2. K2tog around (8 st).
3. Kfb, repeat around (16 st).
4. Kfb, repeat around (32 st).
5. Knit 6 rounds.
6. *K7, kfb* repeat around (36 st).
7. Knit 5 rounds.
8. Stuff head up to top.
9. K2tog, repeat around (18 st).

Leave on needles until face is attached.

Face:

1. On 3.5mm (size 4) needles, cast on 4 st in light brown.
2. Pfb, P2, pfb (6 st).
3. Kfb, k4, kfb (8 st).
4. Pfb, P6, pfb (10 st).
5. Kfb, k8, kfb (12 st).
6. Pfb, p10, pfb (14 st).
7. Add short row – knit to final 3 stitches, wrap and turn, purl to final 3 st, wrap and turn, knit across to end.
8. Purl 1 row.
9. K2tog, k10, k2tog (12 st).
10. Purl 1 row.
11. K2tog, k2tog, k4, k2tog, k2tog (8 st).
12. Cast off in purl.

To attach the face to the head, sew the bottom edge of the face (cast-on edge) to the bottom of head, then sew the top edge of the face (bound-off edge) to the top of the head. While sewing the top edge, stitch a furrow into the brow to give a deranged appearance. Attach safety eyes, pushing through face patch and head before affixing backs. Stuff bottom half of face patch, then stitch down the sides of the face.

To create the mouth, using red yarn, sew five vertical stitches in the mouth position, then one long horizontal stitch over the top.

Close the head:

1. K2tog around (9 st).
2. Add more stuffing if needed.
3. K1, then k2tog around (5 st).
4. Cut yarn, thread onto tapestry needle and run through remaining stitches. Pull firmly to close.

Arms and legs (make 2 of each):

1. On 3.5mm (size 4) needles, cast on 6 st in red (legs) or mid brown (arms) and divide between three needles.
2. Place marker.
3. Knit 12 rounds.
4. K2, kfb, k2, kfb (8 st).
5. Knit 8 rounds (arms) or 6 rounds (legs).

Paws:

1. Divide stitches on 2 needles, work on 4 st one side at a time.
2. In light brown kfb, k2, kfb (6 st).
3. Purl 1 row.
4. Knit 1 row.
5. P2tog, p2, p2tog (4 st).
6. Cast off by knitting 2 together twice and passing stitch over. Cut yarn and run thread through last stitch. Repeat for other side of paw.

Assemble the arms/legs:

Cut four lengths of 9cm (3½in) pipe cleaner and bend over the ends so that they fit inside the limbs, right up to the edge of the paws. Sew the paws together with the pipe cleaner inside.

Ears (make 2):

1. On 3.5mm (size 4) needles, cast on 11 stitches in light brown.
2. Knit 1 row.
3. Purl 1 row.
4. K1 *sl1, k2tog, psso* repeat * to last stitch, k1 (5 st).
5. Cast off in purl.

Fold in half along bound-off edge and sew together to make the ear shape. Attach to sides of head, and oversew around the rims of the ears once attached.

Fez:

1. On 3.5mm (size 4) needles, cast on 18 stitches in red.
2. Knit 3 rows.
3. Purl 1 row.
4. *K1, k2tog* across (12 st).
5. Purl 1 row.
6. Knit 3 rows.
7. *P1, p2tog* across (8 st).

Cut yarn, run through remaining stitches and pull to close. Seam up edges. Using a pair of compasses, draw and cut a 2cm (¾in) diameter disc of thin card. Apply a thin layer of glue and stick to inside top of hat.

Cymbals (make 2):

1. On 3mm (size 3) needles, cast on 5 stitches in yellow.
2. Knit 1 row.
3. Kfb across row (10 st).
4. Knit 1 row.
5. *Kfb, k1* repeat across (15 st).
6. Knit 1 row.
7. *Kfb, k2* repeat across (20 st).
8. Knit 1 row.
9. *Kfb, k3* repeat across (25 st).
10. Knit 1 row.
11. *Kfb, k4* repeat across (30 st).
12. Knit 1 row.
13. Cast off loosely.

You should now have a piece that looks like a pie with a wedge missing. To make the cymbal shape, sew the wedge closed by stitching together the cast-on edge.

Tassel:

Step 1 Wrap a length of gold thread around a ruler four or five times. Thread a needle with a shorter length of gold thread and slip the thread under one edge of the ruler.

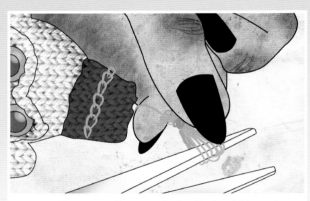

Step 2 Tie at top of loops and slip off ruler. With another length of gold thread, tie around the entire bundle about 5mm (¼in) from the top. Cut through bottom loops and trim to 25mm (1in) long. Sew to the centre top of the fez. Stuff the fez firmly, then, using gold yarn, sew a line of decorative chain stitch about 5mm (¼in) from the base. Stitch the fez to the top of the head at a jaunty angle.

Finishing touches:

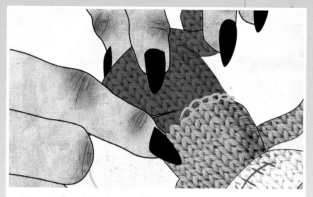

Step 1 Bend the feet and legs and stitch them to the base of the body. Using gold yarn, sew a decorative chain stitch around the top of the pants.

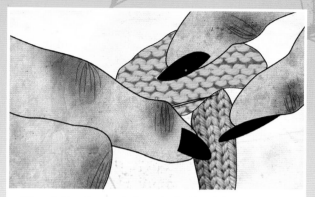

Step 3 Sew the cymbals to the inside of the paws.

Step 2 Bend the paws and arms into position and stitch them securely to the sides of the body.

Ferdy Hand Puppet

Ferdy, an evil, serial-killing dream-monster, has been slaughtering slumbering teens for years, and there's no sign that his hunt is slowing.

With his grotesquely maimed face, his knife-pronged glove, and his ruthless pursuit of sleeping high-school glitterati, Ferdy is a good reason to try and stay awake. However, Ferdy ceases to be scary when you realize that thwarting his murderous intentions is as easy as tricking him into plunging his knifed glove into a large butternut squash. Since he has a creepy habit of scraping those knives along pipes and walls, he is constantly blunting them, and it would take several minutes for him to free himself from a firm gourd. This would give you more than enough time to knock his hat off and run away!

This puppet isn't quite as deadly as a real serial-killing dream-monster, but in the depths of night, it's just as terrifying. Give dozing friends and family a safe scare with your hand puppet and they'll never nap again!

You will need:

- ☠ 4mm (size 6) double-pointed needles (dpns)
- ☠ 3.25mm (size 3) double-pointed needles (dpns)
- ☠ 5mm (size 8) knitting needles
- ☠ DK knitting yarn in red, dark green, brown and flesh
- ☠ Rowan Kidsilk Haze shade 00627 Blood
- ☠ Wash + Filz It! Fine felting yarn in 107 Char brown and 120 Blanket grey
- ☠ Tapestry or yarn needle
- ☠ Polyester toy stuffing
- ☠ 2 x 15mm (⅝in) black safety eyes
- ☠ Small piece of brown felt for glove
- ☠ PVA glue or fabric stiffener

Body:

1. On 4mm (size 6) dpns, cast on 56 stitches and divide between 3 needles. Place stitch marker.
2. Work 5 rounds k2, p2 rib.
3. Change to red and work 5 rounds in stocking stitch.
4. Change to dark green and work 5 rows in stocking stitch.
5. Continue working alternating red and dark green stripes for 30 rows, until there are 7 stripes in total (40 rows including ribbing).
6. Divide into 2 sets of 28 stitches on two needles, with the back seam in the middle of one of the sets of 28 stitches.

'Jogless' stripes

When knitting stripes in the round, changing to a different color creates a visible 'jog' in the fabric where the color changes. To avoid this, knit the first round of the new color as usual. When you reach the end of the round, lift the last stitch of the old color with your right-hand needle and place it on the left-hand needle, then k2tog for the first stitch of the new round. This should make your color changes practically undetectable!

Arms:

The rest of the puppet body is worked flat, working on one set of 28 stitches at a time. Continue to work in stocking stitch throughout.

1. In dark green, cast on 4 stitches at the beginning of the next 2 rows (36 st).
2. Work 3 rows.
3. Change to red, work 2 rows.
4. k2tog, k32, k2tog (34 st).
5. Work 2 rows.
6. Change to dark green, work 5 rows.
7. Change to red, work 2 rows.
8. Cast off 11 stitches at the beginning of the next 2 rows (12 st).

Neck (continue from arms):

9. In dark green, k1, p1 rib for 4 rows.
10. K2tog at beginning of next 6 rows, continuing in k1, p1 rib.
11. Cast off.
12 . Repeat from 1–11 for the other side of the body.

To make up body:

Join body pieces along underside of arms, top edges of arms, and around the neck. Weave in all ends, but leave the ends poking through to the outside of your work – these will be trimmed to give a frayed effect later.

Head:

The head is worked using a strand of flesh-coloured DK and Rowan Kidsilk Haze held together. Work in stocking stitch throughout.

1. On 4mm (size 6) dpns, cast on 24 stitches and divide between needles. Place marker.
2. Work 5 rounds.
3. *K1, kfb* repeat around (36 st).
4. *K5, kfb* repeat around (42 st).
5. Work 20 rounds.
6. K2tog around (21 st).

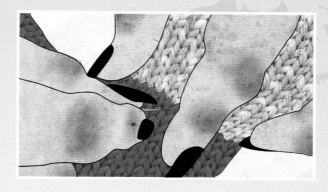

7. K1, k2tog around (14 st).
8. Work 1 round.
9. K2tog around (7 st).
10. Cut yarn, thread onto tapestry needle and run through the remaining stitches. Pull firmly to close the top of the head.

Attach safety eyes and stuff the head firmly, leaving room for fingers. Run a flesh-coloured gathering yarn through the stitches 5 rows from base of the head (this forms the neck). Pull until the neck opening measures 4cm (1½in) in diameter.

Insert fingers into the neck on the body and push into the base of head. Sew the neck edge of the head to the body. Using dark brown felting yarn, make two long stitches for Ferdy's eyebrows. With red yarn, make a long stitch for his mouth.

Collar:

1. On 3.25mm (size 3) needles, cast on 34 stitches in dark green.
2. Work 3 rows in k1, p1 rib.
3. Cast off in rib.

Wrap the collar piece around the neck and sew along the short edges. With the seam at the back of the head, sew around the top and bottom to secure in place.

Hand (make 1 in flesh, 1 in brown):

1. On 4mm (size 6) needles, cast on 28 stitches in flesh or brown
2. In stocking stitch, work 2 rows.
3. K1, k2tog, k9, s1, k1, psso, k2tog, k9, s1, k1, psso, k1 (24 st).
4. Purl 1 row.
5. K1, k2tog, k7, s1, k1, psso, k2tog, k7, s1, k1, psso, k1 (20 st).
6. P1, p2tog, p5, s1, k1, psso, p2tog, p5, s1, k1, psso, p1 (16 st).
7. K1, k2tog, k3, s1, k1, psso, k2tog, k3, s1, k1, psso, k1 (12 st).
8. Cast off in purl

Fold the hand pieces in half and seam using mattress stitch.

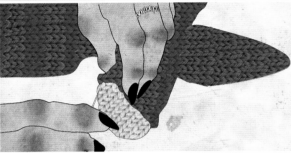

Hat:

Worked in stocking stitch throughout.

1. On 5mm (size 8) needles, cast on 54 stitches in Wash + Filz It! brown.
2. Purl 1 row.
3. *K2, k2tog, k2* repeat across (45 st).
4. Purl 1 row.
5. *K3, k2tog* repeat across (36 st).
6. Purl 1 row.
7. Work 14 rows, ending purl row.
8. K1, k2tog, k1, k2tog, k6, *k2tog, k1* four times, k6, k2tog, k1, k2tog, k1 (28 st).
9. Work 3 rows.
10. K2tog, k2tog, k6, *k2tog* four times, k6, k2tog, k2tog (20 st).
11. Purl 1 row.
12. Cast off.

To make up the hat, sew up the back seam and across crown using mattress stitch. To felt the hat, place it in a pillowslip and secure with an elastic band, then run through a regular cycle in your washing machine. Pull into shape while still damp and leave to dry completely. When dry, stuff lightly with polyester toy stuffing and sew to Ferdy's head using a length of Wash + Filz It! brown yarn.

Knives (make 4):

1. On 3.25mm (size 3) dpns, cast on 3 stitches in Wash +
   Filz It! in grey.
2. Work 10 rows I-cord.
3. K2tog, k1.
4. Work 1 row I-cord.
5. Cut yarn, run through remaining stitches and pull tightly.

Assemble knives and glove:

Felt the knife pieces by securing inside a cotton pillowslip and
running through a regular wash in your washing machine. While the
pieces are still damp, saturate them with fabric stiffener or 2 parts
PVA glue to 1 part water solution. Shape the knife pieces into a
slight curve. Place between two pieces of non-stick parchment or
silicone paper, put a board or hardback book on top and weigh
down with more books or heavy weights. Leave the ends of the
knives sticking out from under the board – these ends will be used
to secure the knives to the felt to make the glove.

When the knives are dry, use a pair of sharp scissors to shape the
ends into points. Cut out a 3 x 1cm (1¼ x ⅜in) piece of brown felt.
Sew the knives into place securely on the felt, then sew the felt
piece to the outside of Ferdy's glove hand.

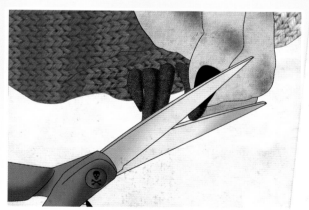

Finishing touches:

To add detail to Ferdy's sweater, sew loose stitches of red and
green yarn around the cuffs, collar and randomly all over the body.
Carefully, using sharp scissors, snip partway through the ply of
the yarn, and brush lightly with your fingers to fray the ends. Be
careful not to snip through any stitches! Trim the woven-in ends
that you pulled through and brush to ravel.

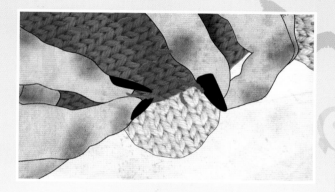

Voodoo Doll Cat Toy

Do you do voodoo? It's not a force to be trifled with, but watching your cat maul this kooky voodoo doll should cheer you up after a bad day, even if you have no particular victim in mind. If you don't have a cat, you could use him as a pincushion. Alternatively, nail him to your housemate's door as a stern reminder of your agreement not to play reggae after 5am.

Hailing principally from Haiti, Louisiana and West Africa, voodoo is a mixture of ancient African traditions and the Christianity that slaves were forced to adopt. The idea of the voodoo doll has mystical and unclear origins, but folk magic practitioners of New Orleans cherish it as a powerful curse. After your sweet kitty gets its teeth and claws into your knitted voodoo toy, you might find your boss looking a little worse for wear...

This doll is worked in reverse stocking stitch, but you don't need to make any special allowances for this. Just knit it in the round and turn the pieces inside out before you stuff them. Catnip is optional, but be warned, it is likely to reduce the toy's lifespan considerably!

You will need:

- ☠ 4.5mm (size 7) double-pointed needles (dpns)
- ☠ Aran weight yarn in beige/oatmeal (Patons Classic Wool Merino in Natural used here)
- ☠ Tapestry needle
- ☠ Polyester toy stuffing
- ☠ Red 4-ply or sock-weight yarn for decoration
- ☠ 2 buttons for the eyes: 1 x 14mm (½in) and 1 x 11mm (⅜in)
- ☠ A small bell
- ☠ Catnip and an old pair of tights (optional!)

Body and head:

1. Cast on 4 stitches for the base of the body. Increase to 8 by knitting into the front and back of each stitch (kfb), then arrange on 3 needles, placing marker.
2. *K1, kfb* repeat to end of round (12 st).
3. Knit 1 round.
4. *K2, kfb* repeat to end of round (16 st).
5. Knit 1 round.
6. *K3, kfb* repeat to end of round (20 st).
7. Knit 1 round.
8. *K4, kfb* repeat to end of round (24 st).

9. Knit 5 rounds.
10. *K4, k2tog* repeat around (20 st).
11. Knit 2 rounds.
12. *K3, k2tog* repeat around (16 st).
13. Knit 2 rounds.
14. *K2, k2tog* repeat around (12 st).
15. Knit 1 round.
16. Increase for head: kfb into every stitch (24 st).
17. Knit 6 rounds.
18. K2tog around (12 st).

With the purl side of the fabric on the outside, stuff the body and head up to the top, placing the bell in the middle of the body. If you are using catnip, use the toe end of an old pair of tights to make a little pouch to put it in. Secure the top with a piece of yarn and stuff it into the centre of the body.

19. P2tog around (6 st).
20. Top up with a little more stuffing, then p2tog around (3 st)
21. Cut yarn, leaving a long tail, thread onto tapestry needle and run through remaining stitches. Pull firmly to close the top of the head.

Legs (make 2):

1. Cast on 3 stitches on 4.5mm (size 7) needles. Increase to 6 st by knitting into front and back of each stitch (kfb) and divide between 3 needles, placing marker.
2. Knit 4 rounds.
3. Kfb, k2, kfb, k2 (8 st).
4. Knit 2 rounds.
5. Kfb, k3, kfb, k3 (10 st).
6. Knit 3 rounds.
7. Kfb, k4, kfb, k4 (12 st).

8. Knit 2 rounds.
9. With purl side out, stuff up to the top.
10. P2tog around (6 st).
11. P2tog around (3 st).
12. Cut yarn, thread onto tapestry needle and run thread through the remaining stitches. Pull firmly to close.

Arms (make 2):

1. Cast on 3 stitches on 4.5mm (size 7) needles. Increase to 6 by knitting into front and back of each stitch (kfb), then divide between three needles. Place marker.
2. Knit 5 rounds.
3. Kfb, k2, kfb, k2 (8 st).
4. Knit 3 rounds.
5. Kfb, k3, kfb, k3 (10 st).
6. Knit 2 rounds.
7. With purl side facing out, stuff up to the top.
8. P2tog around (5 st).
9. Cut yarn, thread end onto tapestry needle and run thread through the remaining stitches. Pull firmly to close.

To assemble:

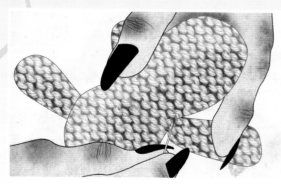

Step 1 Sew arms and legs to body loosely – make sure they are securely attached but try to leave plenty of 'dangle'. Then, with red yarn, sew a few decorative stitches where the limbs join the body.

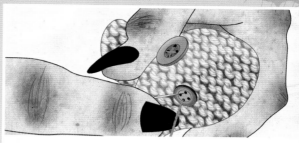

Step 2 Attach the button eyes. Buttons are generally safe to use when making cat toys, but do attach them firmly. If you're concerned that your cat may be the button-eating type, you could use safety eyes. Use any size or colour of buttons that you like. Here, slightly different button sizes/colours were used for each eye to add character.

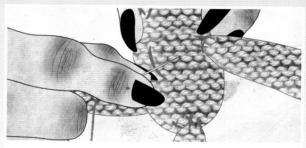

Step 3 Using the red yarn, stitch the mouth in place – a lopsided mouth should leave you feeling suitably avenged. Finally, stitch a red X over your victim's heart. If you like, you could cut out a heart-shaped piece of felt and stitch this in place. Weave in all ends and you're finished! Throw your victim to the lions!

Necronomicon iPad Cosy

"...these enduring creatures may lie dormant but are never truly dead... they may be recalled to active life through the incantations presented in this book. It is through the recitation of these passages that the demons are given licence to possess the living." The Evil Dead (1981)

In his unnerving 1920s tale *The Hound*, H.P. Lovecraft introduced the Necronomicon to successive generations of Gothic horror fans. A grimoire, or magical how-to manual, the Necronomicon instructs its readers in the secrets of divination and summoning supernatural beings. Possibly most famous for its appearance in the film *The Evil Dead*, this terrifying textbook leads hapless hero Ash and his doomed accomplices to summon all manner of demonic entities when they flick through its ancient pages, giving a chilling twist on the old adage, 'don't try this at home' – unless you're knitting your own Necronomicon, that is.

Providing a perfect protective cover for the source of all knowledge, wisdom, and nefarious instructional clips (your iPad), the Necronomicon should also scare friends and family away from your prized igadget. Should you find yourself unable to withstand the lure of games, music, films and general time wasting, remember, it's not your fault – the evil iPad cosy has you possessed!

Adjusting the pattern

If you're not lucky enough to own an iPad, you can adjust this pattern to fit your laptop – measure your laptop width and length in cm, then multiply the width in cm by 1.7, and the length in cm by 2.4. Round up the answer, and then add 2 to the totals to allow for seaming. For example, if your laptop measures 25cm wide by 38cm long:

25 x 1.7 = 42.5
(round up to 43, add 2 for seam = 45)
38 x 2.4 = 91.2
(round up to 92, add 2 for seam = 94)

This tells us we need to cast on 45 stitches and knit 94 rows. Don't forget to make the last 5 rows in k1, p1 rib. The face can be the same size, just position it centrally.

You will need:

- ☠ 5mm (size 8) needles
- ☠ 3.25mm (size 3) double-pointed needles (dpns)
- ☠ 2 x balls Debbie Bliss Donegal Luxury Aran Tweed in shade #04, red, or equivalent yarn to make tension
- ☠ Black felt
- ☠ Tailor's chalk
- ☠ Fabric glue or Copydex
- ☠ 1 x black, old-looking button, about 2cm (¾in) in diameter
- ☠ 1 x iPad

Front and back:

Tension: 17 stitches and 24 rows on 5mm (size 8) needles = 10cm (4in).

1. On 5mm (size 8) needles, cast on 34 stitches.
2. Knit 1 row.
3. K1, p32, k1.
4. Repeat rows 2 and 3 32 times (66 rows in total).
5. Work 5 rows in k1, p1 rib.
6. Cast off loosely.
7. Repeat rows 1–7 to make back panel.

Pin and block each piece to shape. Sew up seams, leaving ribbed edge open.

Face:

On 3.25mm (size 3) needles, cast on 3 stitches and make six lengths of I-cord (see page 25) as detailed below:
- 2 x lengths of 14–16cm (5½–6½in) for the eyes
- 1 x length of 36cm (14in) for the mouth
- 2 x lengths of 9–11cm (3½–4¼in) for the eyebrows
- 1 x length of 13cm (5in) for the brow furrow

To assemble:

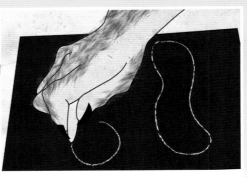

Step 1 Plan your face shapes by playing around with the I-cord on the finished front panel until you find a shape/expression you are happy with. Use the photographs here as a reference, but don't be afraid to give your face its own evil demeanour! Then trace the shapes of your eyes and mouth onto black felt using tailor's chalk and cut out.

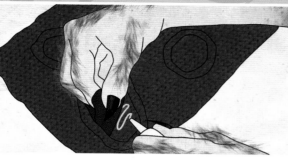

Step 2 With your iPad inside the cosy, use a very thin layer of glue to fix the eye and mouth patches in place on the front of the cosy. If you don't want to use glue near your iPad, you can cut a 25 x 19cm (10 x 7½in) piece of card and slot that in instead. Fixing on the face while the cosy is stretched ensures that your knitting won't distort and look strange when it's finally put to use.

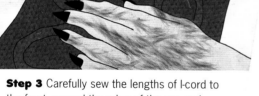

Step 3 Carefully sew the lengths of I-cord to the front, around the edge of the eye and mouth patches. Then sew on the brows and brow furrow.

Button tab:

1. On 3.25mm (size 3) dpns, cast on 6 stitches.
2. Work 12 rows in stocking stitch.
3. K2tog across (3 st).
4. Continue in I-cord for 3.5cm (1½in), cut yarn, and run thread through.
5. Take the cast-off end and secure it to the base of the I-cord to make a loop.

Position the button tab to the inside front of the cosy, with the stocking stitch side uppermost. With your iPad inside the cosy, mark the position of the button on the back panel and sew firmly in place. Now you're ready to summon something from the great beyond! Or you could just check your email.

Shrunken Head in a Jar

Shrinking heads is a messy process. First you remove the skull, then scoop out all the flesh and fat, and fill the cavity with seeds and wood before boiling the skin in water. This fashionable home accessory can then be adorned with decorative beads and hair. Alternatively, skip the decapitation and knit one instead.

Historically taken as trophies of war, shrunken heads originated among the remote Amazonian tribes of Ecuador and Peru. The captured and preserved heads were believed to bestow upon the owner the power of their slain enemy; the lips and eyes of these gruesome specimens were carefully secured with stitches to prevent the spirit from escaping and exacting revenge. Prized by Victorian private collectors and explorers, an authentic shrunken head would have been the crowning glory in any collection of curiosities, guaranteed to pique the morbid curiosity of all who laid eyes upon one.

These shrunken heads are knitted in the round from the neck up. The head is then stuffed before the hair and features are stitched into place. You can use a stitch marker to remind you where the end of the round is, or use the cast-on tail as a visual guide. If you have a large glass cookie jar to display it in, a thick piece of stick inserted into the neck opening will help the head stand up for display. Alternatively, you can squash your shrunken head into a smaller jar for a distorted look. You could even squeeze two or three heads into the same jar for a more terrifying effect!

You will need:

- ☠ 3.75mm (size 5) double-pointed needles (dpns)
- ☠ Brown or dark tan Double Knitting (DK) yarn for head
- ☠ Black or grey fuzzy mohair or 2-ply yarn for hair
- ☠ Polyester fibre toy stuffing
- ☠ 2 x 4-hole buttons for eyes, 18mm (¾in)
- ☠ Felt for lips
- ☠ Tapestry needle
- ☠ Sewing needle and thread
- ☠ Glue
- ☠ Hairspray
- ☠ Large cookie jar for display
- ☠ Stick

To make the head:

1. Cast on 18 stitches and divide between 3 needles. Join for knitting in the round.
2. Knit 6 rounds.
3. K1 *k1f&b, k2* repeat from * to * until 2 stitches remain, k1f&b, k1 (24 st).
4. Knit 1 round.
5. K1f&b, repeat to end of round (48 st).
6. Knit 11 rounds.
7. K2, k2tog, k2tog, knit to last 6 stitches then ssk, ssk, k2 (44 st).
8. Knit 2 rounds.
9. K2tog to end of round (22 st).
10. K2, k2tog, knit to last 4 stitches then ssk, k2 (20 st).
11. K2 tog to end of round (10 st).
12. Cut yarn and thread through remaining stitches, pulling gently to close the top of the head.

To attach the hair:

Stuff and shape the head evenly and firmly. Using a tapestry needle and yarn the same colour as the yarn for the hair, sew large (2.5cm/1in) backstitches around the crown of the head, marking the hairline.

For each 2.5cm (1in) backstitch, cut ten to twelve 30cm (12in) lengths of mohair (or whatever yarn you are using for the hair). Thread these lengths through the backstitch until the stitch lies in the center and smooth out the yarn evenly so that it 'fills' the whole stitch. Using a regular sewing needle and cotton, sew the section of hair into place, working parallel to the original backstitch.

Repeat for each section, working all the way around the head until all hair is in place. The hair can then be gathered up and secured into a loose ponytail on top of the head. When you have a style you're happy with, you can give it a light spritz of hairspray to keep it in place.

Decorate the head:

Step 1 To finish, you can accessorize your shrunken head with chicken bones and feathers threaded into the hair.

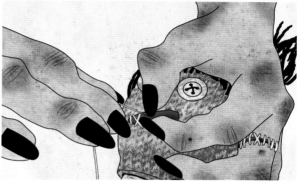

Step 2 Cut a thin strip of felt for the lips and glue it into place. When the glue is dry, sew over the mouth with several long stitches using a lighter coloured yarn.

Step 3 Using a contrasting yarn or thread, sew the buttons in place for the eyes. If you like, you can sew a large X over each button to enhance the effect of the eyes being sewn shut.

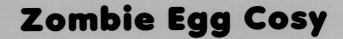

Zombie Egg Cosy

It's a common misconception that zombies eat brains. Unfortunately for hungry zombies, their jaws are simply not strong enough to bite through that thick skull of yours. Besides, destroy the brain and you destroy the zombie convert – if they went around eating our brains, the undead epidemic would never get off the ground. *Return Of The Living Dead* has a lot to answer for.

Existing in mythology from Haiti to Tibet, Africa to Eastern Europe, the zombie is a scary staple in the wholesome horror diet – and definitely part of a complete breakfast. Here is your chance to smash a zombie brain in, with this open-topped boiled egg cosy. Breakfast has never been so much gruesome fun! Bring your blunt weapon (spoon) down directly on his head and think of it as practice for the coming apocalypse.

This cosy will fit a medium-sized egg, but should be stretchy enough to accommodate a larger size, unless you have a penchant for ostrich eggs. Any eggcup will do, but find one with legs if you can!

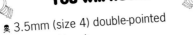

You will need:

- ☠ 3.5mm (size 4) double-pointed needles (dpns)
- ☠ DK yarn in pale green and dark red
- ☠ 2 x white/pearlescent, flat-fronted buttons (1 x 10mm and 1 x 12mm were used here)
- ☠ Small scraps of black and red felt
- ☠ Tapestry needle
- ☠ Sewing needle
- ☠ Sharp scissors
- ☠ Permanent marker

Body:

1. Cast on 27 stitches in light green, using a stretchy cast on. Divide onto 3 needles and place marker.
2. Purl 2 rounds.
3. Knit 10 rounds.
4. *K1, k2tog* repeat around (18 st).
5. Knit 1 round.
6. *K1, k2tog* repeat around (12 st).
7. Knit 1 round.
8. K2tog around (8 stitches).
9. Cut yarn, thread onto tapestry needle and run thread through remaining stitches. Pull to close.

Arms (make 2):

1. Cast on 3 stitches.
2. Work 8 rows of I-cord.
3. K1, kfb, k1 (4 st).
4. Knit 1 round in I-cord.
5. Cast off.

To finish:

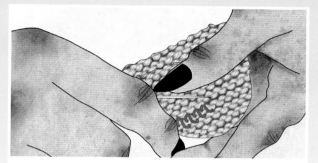

Step 1 Count 10 rows up from base of work (not including purl rows), around 3.5cm (1½in). Take a length of pale green yarn and separate two of the threads from the ply, to make a thinner length of yarn for sewing. Thread the sewing needle with yarn and sew carefully around the top, making sure to 'catch' all of the knit stitches as you sew. Sew round a number of times to secure.

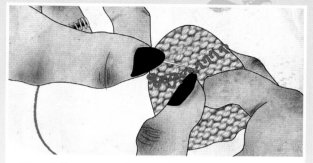

Step 2 Turn your work wrong (purl) side out. Using dark red DK yarn, sew a line of chain stitch around the inside, working over your green stitching. Your stitches shouldn't poke through to the right (knit) side, so be careful to pick up only a few threads from the inside as you sew.

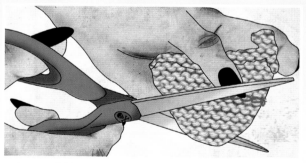

Step 3 With a pair of small, sharp scissors, boldly cut the top off your cosy just above the line of chain stitch. Turn the cosy right side out, and use your sewing needle to fray the cut edges. Carefully snip through a few of the threads on your red chain stitch – not all the way through! You don't want it to unravel completely, just look a little ragged.

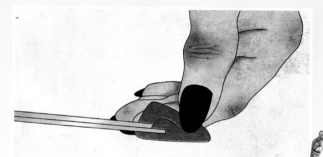

Step 4 Cut a small triangle of red felt, and cut a smaller triangle from the centre for the mouth. Glue into place. For the eyes, cut out two ovals of black felt, and snip a small slit in them for the shank of your button. Sew the felt-backed buttons firmly in place – you can also glue the felt to the face if you like. This will help it lie flatter once it's on the egg.

Step 5 Finally, stitch the arms in place and weave in all the yarn ends. Slip over your perfectly boiled egg and arm yourself with a spoon – it's brain smashing time!

Freak Show Finger Puppets

Knit an array of weird and wonderful freak show finger puppets! Entice, amaze, entrance, and perhaps appal, those who seek a peek at the freak.

The freak show was an indispensable attraction for many travelling circuses in nineteenth- and early twentieth-century America. Also recorded in Europe as early at 1630, these sideshows featured bearded ladies, conjoined twins, the heavily tattooed or pierced, and even fire-eating or sword-swallowing acts. Average townsfolk gathered in large numbers to see the weird and wonderful world of the 'freak'. The most famous and best-loved of these attractions remains Joseph Merrick, known as The Elephant Man, whose late nineteenth-century appearances in London ultimately revealed a common but tragic human story behind the glitz of the show. Despite its fall from grace, the freak show is actually re-emerging today as performers proudly display their interesting oddities and unique skills.

While it's difficult to create just a small selection of individuals from the rich array of characters that have graced the much-loved freakshow stage – with such gems as the Hairy family of Mandalay, Camel Girl and Lobster Boy to choose from – here is a selection of tributes to these curious characters of yore.

Lion-faced Boy's body:

Use bobbins for different coloured yarns (2 bobbins for main colour, 1 for contrast colour) and twist yarns together at colour changes to prevent holes. On 3.25mm (size 3) needles, cast on 20 stitches in light blue yarn (mc).

1. Knit 1 row.
2. Knit 9 mc, 2 white (cc), 9 mc.
3. Purl 9 mc, 2 cc, 9 mc.
4. Repeat row 2.
5. Repeat row 3.
6. Knit 8 mc, 4 cc, 8 mc.
7. Purl 8 mc, 4 cc, 8 mc.
8. Repeat row 6.
9. Repeat row 7.
10. Knit 7 mc, 6 cc, 7 mc.
11. Purl 7 mc, 6 cc, 7 mc.
12. Knit 2 mc, ssk in mc, knit 3 mc, 6 cc, 3 mc, k2tog in mc, knit 2 mc (18 st).
13. Purl 5 mc, 8 cc, 5 mc.
14. Knit 2 mc, ssk in mc, knit 1 mc, 8 cc, 1 mc, k2tog in mc, knit 2 mc (16 st).
15. Purl 4 mc, 8 cc, 4 mc.
16. Knit 1 mc, ssk in mc, knit 1 mc, 8 cc, 1 mc, k2tog in mc, knit 1 mc (14 st).

Head:

1. In flesh, purl 2, ssp, purl 6, p2tog, purl 2 (12 st).
2. K2, kfb in every stitch until last 2 stitches, k2 (20 st).
3. Beginning purl row, work 7 rows in stocking stitch, ending purl row.
4. K2tog, repeat to end (10 st).
5. Purl 1 row.
6. Cut yarn leaving a long tail, run yarn through remaining stitches and pull to close top of head.

Arms (make 2):
1. On 3.25mm (size 3) dpns, cast on 3 st in mc.
2. Work 7 rows of I-cord.
3. Switch to flesh and work 3 rows for hands.
4. Cast off.

Collar:
1. In mc, cast on 14 st on 3.25mm (size 3) needles.
2. Cast off.

To assemble:
Seam up the back of the body and head using mattress stitch. Stuff the head with a small amount of polyester stuffing, leaving room for your finger! Attach the safety eyes. Sew the collar in place and attach the arms.

Hair:
Lion-faced Boy's hair is made and attached in six sections, but all are made in the same way. For the brow, cut nine lengths of 20cm (8in) light brown yarn. Lay one out horizontally in front of you and attach the remaining pieces one at a time, by folding in half, tucking the folded end under the horizontal strand and pulling the ends through the loop.

With a sewing thread and needle, attach the brow piece with strands pointing upwards, just above the eyes. Now, make two cheek sections of hair by cutting seven 20cm (8in) lengths of yarn and assembling them as above. Sew into place. Using a length of red yarn, make a stitch for the mouth as shown. Then, make the beard in the same way as the hair, with six 20cm (8in) lengths of yarn. Stitch in place. Finally, make the nose piece with two strands of 20cm (8in) yarn and stitch into place with light brown wool and a tapestry needle to make the nose. Smooth and arrange all hair sections into place, trim as required to neaten ends and spray lightly with hairspray to hold in place.

Bearded Lady's body:
1. In lilac (mc), cast on 20 stitches on 3.25mm (size 3) needles.
2. Knit 2 rows.
3. Beginning with a purl row, work 7 rows in stocking stitch.
4. Knit 2, ssk, knit, 12, k2tog, knit 2 (18 st).
5. Purl 1 row.
6. Change yarn colour to flesh, knit 2, ssk, knit 10, k2tog, knit 2 (16 st).
7. Purl 1 row.
8. Knit 1, ssk, knit 10, k2tog, knit 1 (14 st).

Head:
1. In flesh, purl 2, ssp, purl 6, p2tog, purl 2 (12 st).
2. K2, kfb in every stitch until last 2 stitches, K2 (20 st).
3. Beginning purl row, work 7 rows in stocking stitch, ending purl row.
4. K2tog, repeat to end (10 st).
5. Purl 1 row.
6. Cut yarn, leaving a long tail, run yarn through the remaining stitches and pull to close the top of the head.

Arms (make 2):
1. On 3.25mm (size 3) dpns, cast on 3 st in mc.
2. Work 3 rows of I-cord.
3. Switch to flesh and work 7 rows.
4. Cast off.

To assemble:
Seam up the back of the body and head using mattress stitch. Stuff the head with polyester stuffing, leaving room for your finger! Attach the arms. Using candy pink yarn and the crochet hook, work crochet picot edging (see page 25) around the bottom of the skirt – single crochet into the edge of the fabric. Chain 3, single crochet twice into first chain, then single crochet into fabric again and continue.

String seed beads onto an 20cm (8in) length of sewing thread until the strung beads measure 11cm (4¼in) in length. Tie the loose thread ends together and trim.

Hair:

Cut out a 6 x 20cm (2½ x 8in) piece of corrugated cardboard. Fold in half lengthways to make a double thickness card measuring 6 x 10cm (2½ x 4in). Using dark brown yarn and starting at one end, wrap yarn around the card in a single thickness, until you reach the end. Cut the yarn and hold in place.

Using a sewing needle and thread, sew across the top of the wrapped yarn to hold the strands together. It's best to go back and forth a few times to ensure it's secure. Carefully slide the yarn off the cardboard and cut through the bottom loops to make your wig.

Divide the hairpiece into three sections and sew firmly to the head. Curl the back section under by wrapping it around the barrel of a pen and saturating with hairspray. Leave to dry before removing the pen.

Take the two side sections and gather them together at the back – tie in place with a length of brown yarn. Thread the tapestry needle with dark brown yarn and carefully sew each section of hair into place. Add a few large stitches around the face to make a neat hairline, then carefully trim the hair at the back if necessary. Spray lightly with hairspray to fix in place.

To finish:

Using a short length of red yarn, make a stitch for the mouth. With the same dark brown yarn used for the hair, sew the beard by making long vertical stitches – build up gradually as you go, layering stitches on top of one another.

Elephant Man

In black (mc), cast on 20 stitches on 3.25mm (size 3) needles. Use bobbins for different coloured yarns (2 bobbins for main colour, 1 for contrast colour) and twist yarns together at colour changes to prevent holes.

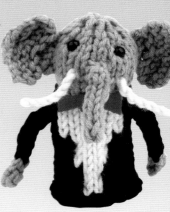

1. Knit 1 row.
2. Knit 9 mc, 2 white (cc), 9 mc.
3. Purl 9 mc, 2 cc, 9 mc.
4. Repeat row 2.
5. Repeat row 3.
6. Knit 8 mc, 4 cc, 8 mc.
7. Purl 8 mc, 4 cc, 8 mc.
8. Repeat row 6.
9. Repeat row 7.
10. Knit 7 mc, 6 cc, 7 mc.
11. Purl 7 mc, 6 cc, 7 mc.
12. Knit 2 mc, ssk in mc, knit 3 mc, 6 cc, 3 mc, k2tog in mc, knit 2 mc (18 st).
13. Purl 5 mc, 8 cc, 5 mc.
14. Knit 2 mc, ssk in mc, knit 1 mc, 8 cc, 1 mc, k2tog in mc, knit 2 mc (16 st).
15. Purl 4 mc, 8 cc, 4 mc.
16. Knit 1 mc, ssk in mc, knit 1 mc, 8 cc, 1 mc, k2tog in mc, knit 1 mc (14 st).

Head (continued from the body):

17. In grey, purl 2, ssp, purl 6, p2tog, purl 2 (12 st).
18. K2, kfb in every stitch until last 2 stitches, k2 (20 st).
19. Beginning purl row, work 7 rows in stocking stitch, ending purl row.

20. K2tog, repeat to end (10 st).
21. Purl 1 row.
22. Cut yarn, leaving a long tail, run yarn through the remaining stitches and pull to close the top of the head.

Arms (make 2):

1. On 3.25mm (size 3) dpns, cast on 3 st in mc.
2. Work 7 rows of I-cord.
3. Switch to grey and work 3 rows for hands.
4. Cast off.

Collar:

1. In mc, cast on 14 st on 3.25mm (size 3) needles.
2. Cast off.

Trunk:

1. In grey, cast on 4 stitches on 3.25mm (size 3) dpns.
2. Work 7 rows of I-cord.
3. Cut yarn, run through stitches and pull firmly.

Ears (make 2):

1. In grey, cast on 4 stitches on 3.25mm (size 3) needles. Work in garter stitch throughout.
2. Kfb in every stitch (8 st).
3. Knit 1 row.
4. Kfb, k6, kfb (10 st).
5. Knit 1 row.
6. K4, k2tog, k4 (9 st).
7. K4, k2tog, k3 (8 st).
8. K2tog across row (4 st).
9. Knit 1 row.
10. Cast off.

Tusks (make 2):

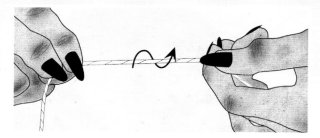

Step 1 Take a 50cm (1½ft) length of white yarn and hold both ends in one hand. Place your finger in the loop, pull the thread taut and then rotate your finger repeatedly to twist the two strands together.

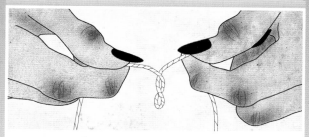

Step 2 Once tightly twisted, hold both ends of the yarn firmly. Placing a finger in the middle of the twisted length to hold it taut, bring both ends together; the yarn will twist around itself to create a short rope effect. Use a bulldog clip or similar to hold the twist and glue or sew to prevent fraying at 5cm (2in) from the end. Tie a knot at around 2.5cm (1in); this will allow 2cm (¾in) of trunk to stick out from the face once threaded through. Trim after the knot.

To assemble:

Seam up back of body and head. Stuff the head with polyester fibre stuffing, leaving room for your finger! Attach safety eyes. Sew collar, arms, ears and trunk into place. For the bow tie, cut two pieces of red felt. Fold a small rectangular piece of felt around the middle to make the knot of the bow. Secure with fabric or contact glue.

Creepy Clown Cushion Cover

'I'm every nightmare you've ever had. I'm your worst dream come true. I'm everything you ever were afraid of.'
Pennywise the Clown, *It* (1990)

One in seven people suffer with Coulrophobia, a fear of clowns – that's a lot of people. Perhaps they're right to be scared. After all, some clowns are truly evil, especially if you believe legendarily creepy author Stephen King and Tim Curry's insomnia-inducing performance in *IT*.

This widespread public anxiety in the face of white make-up and garish hair was best expressed by character Bart Simpson in the popular animated TV show, *The Simpsons*. Gifted a new headboard in the shape of a clown, Bart refuses to slumber, murmuring, 'can't sleep, clown will eat me'. The sound bite resonated with millions of viewers, inspiring bumper stickers, t-shirts and even an Alice Cooper song.

Clowns truly are an indispensable part of the horror character arsenal, with the power to reduce well-adjusted adults to the emotional strength of six-year-old children. If you know someone with a fear of clowns, reassure them they are in good company... then knit them this creepy cushion cover to help them get over it.

Don't be put off by the intarsia in this project – while it can seem tricky to begin with, as long as you prepare well by winding your yarn onto bobbins before you start (see page 23), you shouldn't have too many problems with tangles.

Tension: 20 stitches and 30 rows = 10cm (4in) square.
Worked in stocking stitch throughout.

Front:

On 4mm (size 6) needles, cast on 60 stitches in black.
Working from bobbins, knit the front piece from the chart
(see page 124) using the intarsia method. Ensure that yarn
tension is kept even throughout and new colors are twisted
together where necessary.

Large back piece:

1. On 4mm (size 6) needles, cast on 60 stitches in black.
2. Work 8 rows black.
3. Change to blue, work 8 rows.
4. Change to black, work 8 rows.
5. Change to pink, work 8 rows.
6. Change to black, work 8 rows.
7. Change to white, work 8 rows.
8. Change to black, knit 1 row.
9. Work 6 rows k1p1 rib.
10. Cast off in rib.

Small back piece:

1. On 4mm (size 6) needles, cast on 60 stitches in pink.
2. Work 8 rows.
3. Change to pink, work 8 rows.
4. Change to black, work 8 rows.
5. Change to blue, work 8 rows.
6. Change to black, work 1 row.
7. Work 4 rows k1, p1 rib.
8. Make buttonhole – k1, p1 for 29, cast off 2, k1,
   p1 for 29 (58 st).
9. K1, p1 for 29, cast on 2, k1, p1 for 29 (60 st).
10. Work 3 more rows in k1, p1 rib.
11. Cast off in rib.

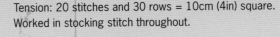

You will need:

☠ 4mm (size 6) needles
☠ Double knitting (DK) yarn in black,
    white, pink, red and blue
☠ 2 x white buttons for eyes
☠ White button for back fastening
☠ Tapestry needle
☠ 25.5-cm (10-in) square cushion pad

To assemble:

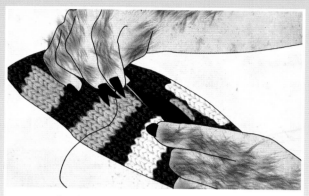

Step 1 Carefully block all pieces (see page 21). With right sides out, sew the large back piece to the front piece. The cast-on edge should be at the bottom, with the rib edge at the top.

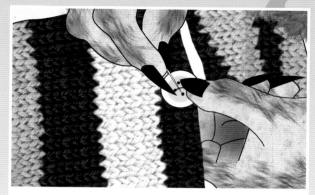

Step 2 Sew the small back piece in place – the rib pieces should overlap to create an envelope opening for the cushion cover. Sew the button to the middle of the large back piece.

Step 3 To finish, make pompoms to decorate the corners of the cushion (see page 27) – you can make as many or as few as you like, but two or three in each corner will work well. Sew the pompoms in place and sew decorative buttons onto the eyes. Stuff your cushion pad into the cover and fasten the button.

Monster Merry-go-Round

There's something creepy about a fairground carousel. Maybe it's the wild faces of the galloping horses, or the distorted, windswept strains of its mechanical pipe organ music. This project is an interpretation of a fairground carousel from another dimension. Roll up and take a ride if you dare!

Famously featured in Ray Bradbury's book *Something Wicked This Way Comes* and Hitchcock's suspenseful thriller, *Strangers on a Train*, the creepy carousel is another seemingly innocent childhood diversion that actually oozes ominous dread. Whether it's a supernatural spell that turns you old or a fast-moving murder weapon, the carousel spells doom for its patrons. Once you climb aboard, there's no way off until the ride slows down. Whatever you encounter on the Monster Merry-go-Round, there's no escape...

This carousel is very customizable – you could make the canopy in black and white and hang it with LED ghosts for a unique Halloween decoration. Or add more monsters in different colours, shapes and sizes – whatever takes your fancy!

You will need:

- ☠ 4mm (size 6) needles
- ☠ 4.5mm (size 7) double pointed needles (dpns) or a 4.5mm (size 7) 40–60cm (16–24in) circular needle
- ☠ 3.25mm (size 3) needles
- ☠ 3.25mm (size 3) double-pointed needles (dpns)
- ☠ 2mm (size 0) needles
- ☠ 8 x 7.5mm black safety eyes
- ☠ DK (Double Knitting) yarn in red, yellow and green
- ☠ Tapestry or yarn needle
- ☠ Mohair or sock-weight yarn in green (Rowan Kidsilk Haze in Jelly was used here)
- ☠ White felt
- ☠ Fabric glue or Copydex
- ☠ Gold or other decorative thread/ yarn (Rowan Lurex Shimmer in Gold was used here)
- ☠ Polyester toy stuffing
- ☠ Aluminium modelling wire (at least 3mm/9-gauge thickness)
- ☠ Duct tape

Canopy:

The canopy is made from eight knitted segments seamed together – four red and four yellow, with a lightweight frame made from aluminium wire to keep it in shape. You could use a circular hoop of strong cardboard if you can't get your hands on any sturdy enough wire.

1. On 4mm (size 6) needles, cast on 1 stitch in red or yellow.
2. Increase to 4 st by knitting into stitch 4 times knitwise.
3. Beginning purl, work 3 rows in stocking stitch.
4. Kfb, k2, kfb (6 st).
5. Purl 1 row.
6. Knit 1 row.
7. Purl 1 row.
8. Kfb, k4, kfb (8 st).
9. Purl 1 row.
10. Knit 1 row.
11. Purl 1 row.
12. Kfb, k6, kfb (10 st).
13. Purl 1 row.
14. Knit 1 row.
15. Purl 1 row.
16. Kfb, k8, kfb (12st).
17. Purl 1 row.
18. Knit 1 row.
19. Purl 1 row.
20. Kfb, k10, kfb (14 st).
21. Work 11 rows straight, ending purl row.
22. Place on stitch holder.

Repeat for seven more segments, making four red and four yellow in total. Seam them together as you go. When you have sewn all of the segments together, place all the live stitches onto 4.5mm (size 7) dpns, or a circular needle. You should now have 112 stitches on your needles.

23. Using yellow yarn, join for knitting in the round, place stitch marker and kfb into first stitch. Continue first round in knit.
24. Purl (to form ridge).
25. Knit 1 row.
26. Purl 1 row.
27. Change to red, knit.
28. Purl 1 row.
29. Change to yellow, knit.

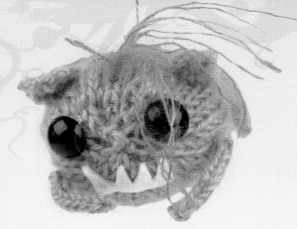

30. Purl 1 row.
31. Knit 1 row.
32. Picot edging: cast off 2 stitches *slip stitch from RH needle onto left, cast on 2 stitches (cable cast on), cast off 4 stitches* repeat from * to * until 1 stitch remains. Cast this stitch off.
33. Weave in all yarn ends.

Monsters (make 4):
Body

1. On 3.25mm (size 3) needles, cast on 6 stitches in green.
2. Purl 1 row.
3. Kfb in every stitch (12 st).
4. Purl 1 row.
5. Kfb in every stitch (24 st).
6. Work 11 rows in stocking stitch, ending purl row.
7. *K1, kfb* repeat from * to * around (36 st).
8. Work 7 rows in stocking stitch, ending purl row.
9. K2tog across (18 st).
10. Purl 1 row.
11. K2tog across (9 st).
12. P2tog, p2tog, p1, p2tog, p2tog (5 st).
13. Cut yarn, leaving a long tail. Run through remaining stitches and pull tight.

Beginning at the cast-off end, sew up the seam in mattress stitch until you reach halfway. Fix the safety eyes in place, and then continue to sew the seam closed, stuffing as you go. Weave in yarn ends.

Legs (make 4 for each monster):
1. On 3.25mm (size 3) dpns, cast on 3 stitches in green.
2. Work 2.5cm (1in) of I-cord.
3. Cut yarn leaving long tail, run through remaining stitches and pull tight.

Sew the legs to the body; pull any remaining threads gently through the body and out of the back to form the tail.

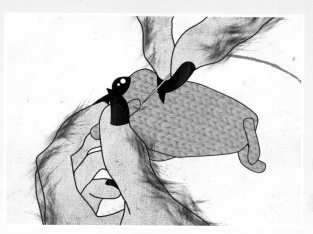

Ears (make 2 for each monster):
1. On 2mm (size 0) needles, cast on 4 stitches in green.
2. Knit 3 rows in garter stitch.
3. K2tog, k2tog (2 st).
4. K2tog (1 st).
5. Cut yarn, leaving long tail, run thread through.

Sew ears to body. Pull remaining threads gently through body and out of the back to form the tail.

The mane:
To make the mane, take seven 15cm (6in) lengths of mohair yarn, fold in half, and thread the folded end through a yarn needle. Pull through between stitches in the centre top of the head, remove the needle and then pull the two cut ends through the loop to secure the tuft of hair.

Repeat this process seven or eight times. You can also add a few strands of mohair to the tail. Trim the mane and tail. Finally, cut a zigzag piece of white felt and glue to the face to make the teeth.

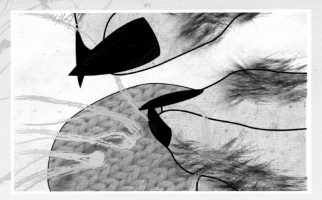

To assemble:

Step 1 Cut a piece of aluminium modelling wire to fit around the circumference of the canopy, at the point just before you started the section that was knitted in the round. Carefully bend the wire into a circle and secure the cut ends with duct tape. Stitch the wire to the underneath of the canopy using red or yellow yarn and a yarn needle.

Step 2 Cut four 20cm (8in) lengths of gold thread, tie a knot in each one, and use a sharp yarn needle to pull the thread through the centre of each monster to make a hanging support. Cut off the loose tail underneath. Tie the monsters to the aluminium frame using the support threads, ensuring they are evenly spaced and hang at the same length.

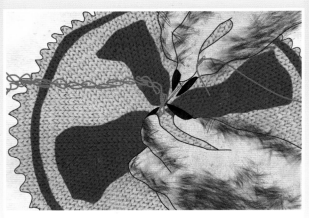

Step 3 Make a loose length of I-cord about 30cm (12in) long. You can also use the 3-pin wheel on a Clover Wonder Knitter to make this. Secure this to the top of the carousel to make a hanging loop. Finally, make a small red pompom and fix it onto the top of the canopy in the centre. Your carousel is ready to hang!

Light-up Ghost

Ghosts have a subtle malevolence that sets them apart from other monsters. A good ghost story needs no splintering bones and buckets of blood, just a sense of creeping dread. Ghosts are the footsteps in a darkened hallway... the shadow behind the curtain... the knocking in the walls. They have existed in our imaginations since the beginning of humanity, and who knows? Perhaps they will be here long after we are gone.

The classic ghost is a white, floating sheet, an image that stems from traditional burial shrouds. Nineteenth-century theatres needed a way to distinguish the dead from the living on stage and the sheet became a recognized trope of theatrical ghost performances. Although the bed-sheet ghost has long since lost its scare appeal to anyone more than four years old, think of it as vintage – the older the phantom, the more powerful it is...

Ward off roaming spirits (or attract them! I make no promises) with these little knitted ghosts. Lit from within with LEDs, they make great Halloween decorations – make a whole line of them for your mantelpiece or string them up into a mobile for maximum impact.

You will need:

- ☠ 3.75mm (size 5) double-pointed needles (dpns)
- ☠ DK yarn in white
- ☠ 2 x 10mm (⅜in) black safety eyes
- ☠ D3 (3mm) crochet hook
- ☠ White table-tennis ball
- ☠ 10mm white diffused LED
- ☠ Cr2032 coin cell battery
- ☠ Sticky tape or electrical tape
- ☠ Polyester fibre toy stuffing

The ghost:

1. Cast on 36 stitches and divide for knitting in the round. Place marker.
2. Knit 3 rounds.
3. *K4, k2tog* around (30 st).
4. Knit 2 rounds.
5. *K3, k2tog* around (24 st).
6. Knit 10 rounds.
7. *K2, k2tog* around (18 st).
8. Knit 1 round.
9. K1 *k2tog* around, k1 (10 st).
10. Knit 1 round.
11. K1 *k2tog* around, k1 (6 st).
12. Knit 1 round.
13. *K1, k2tog* around (4 st).
14. Knit 2 rounds.
15. K1, k2tog , k1 (3 st).
16. Cut yarn and run through remaining stitches, pull to close.

Using white DK yarn and the crochet hook, work a crochet picot edging around the bottom of the ghost (see page 25). To do this, single crochet into the edge of the fabric. Chain 3, single crochet twice into first chain, then single crochet into fabric again. Continue around.

To assemble:

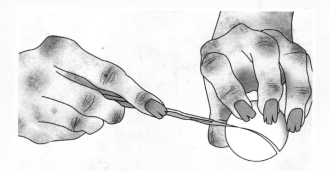

Step 1 Weave in yarn ends. Using a craft knife, carefully cut the bottom off the table-tennis ball.

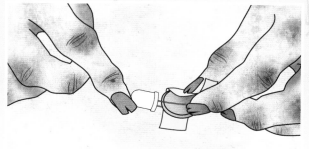

Step 2 Take the LED and trim the ends of the legs so the longest (positive) leg lies flush with the edge of the battery, with the negative leg a fraction shorter. Tape in place, long leg to positive.

Step 3 Turn the ghost upside-down, drop the LED inside and use a small amount of polyester stuffing to keep it in place.

Step 4 Push inside the body of the ghost and mark the position of the eyes with a pencil through the knitted fabric. Remove ball and cut two small 'X' shapes to allow you to push the eye through. Push the ball back up inside and secure in place by pushing the eyes through the Xs.

Abominable Snowman

The Abominable Snowman, or Yeti, is Bigfoot's white-haired cousin. Roaming the chilly mountains of the Himalayas, this elusive creature leaves little evidence of its presence, except the odd huge footprint.

Interest in the Abominable Snowman peaked in the 1950s, when several Everest expedition parties reported seeing mysterious footprints high up on the mountain, bringing Yeti-hunting parties out in force. Definitive evidence was never presented, but to this day, determined Yeti hunters live in hope of proving the existence of this man–monster, once and for all.

Fur stitch, which is used for this particular monster, can be tricky to get to grips with at first, but you'll soon be working loops like a pro. It's a great stitch to learn and worth the effort! If you're really baffled, look up an instructional video on the Internet or ask someone in the know to show you the ropes; it's much easier once you've actually seen it. For a different effect, you can cut the loops to make the fur lie flatter, and even brush the yarn with a wire brush for an extra-furry effect.

You will need:

- ☠ 4mm (size 6) double-pointed bamboo needles (dpns)
- ☠ 3 balls DK yarn in ecru/natural (Sirdar Eco Wool in ecru is used here)
- ☠ White tooth-shaped beads (white turquoise chips are used here) or white DK yarn
- ☠ 7-count plastic canvas
- ☠ Polyester fibre toy stuffing
- ☠ 2 x 9mm (⅜in) black toy safety eyes
- ☠ Black felt
- ☠ Tapestry needle
- ☠ Ecru or white mohair (Debbie Bliss Angel in ecru used here)
- ☠ Black cotton thread

Bamboo needles

Attempting the fur stitch in the round (right), on slippery metal needles may prove difficult, so you could try using bamboo needles as the stitches slip off the needles much less readily.

Fur stitch

The legs and arms for the Abominable Snowman are worked in fur stitch, which is worked over 4 rows. There are several variations on how to create the fur, or loop, stitch, and any one of them will work equally well here; however, the one used for this project is as follows:

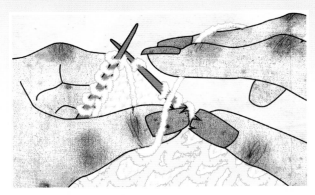

1. Knit 1 row.
2. *K1, k1 but before completing new stitch (keeping stitch on left-hand needle) bring yarn forward, pass yarn around left thumb to make a loop, yb, and knit into the stitch again, slip it off the needle and pass the first stitch over. From here onwards, this will be referred to in the pattern as Make Loop (ML).* Repeat to end.
3. Knit 1 row.
4. *ML, k1* repeat.

These four rows equal one repeat fur stitch.

Legs (make 2):

On 4mm (size 6) needles, cast on 5 stitches in ecru DK and divide the stitches for knitting in the round.

1. Knit 1 round.
2. Kfb in every stitch (10 st).
3. Knit 1 round.
4. Kfb in every stitch (20 st).
5. Knit 1 round.
6. K1, kfb around (30 st).
7. Knit 1 round.
8. K2, kfb around (40 st).

9. Knit 1 round.
10. Work fur stitch for 4 repeats (16 rows).
11. Cut out a 2in (5cm) diameter circle of plastic canvas, turn leg inside out and sew securely to the inside base of the foot. Turn right-side out and lightly stuff the foot.
12. *K4, k2tog* 6 times, k4 (34 st).
13. Work 2nd, 3rd and 4th rounds of fur stitch.
14. *K3, k2tog* 6 times, k4 (28 st).
15. Work 2nd, 3rd and 4th rounds of fur stitch.
16. Work fur stitch for 4 repeats.
17. *K2, k2tog* 6 times, k4 (22 st).
18. Work 2nd, 3rd and 4th rounds of fur stitch.
19. Work fur stitch for 3 repeats.
20. *K1, k2tog* 6 times, k4 (16 st).
21. Work 2nd, 3rd and 4th rounds of fur stitch.
22. Work fur stitch for 2 repeats.

Body/head:

When both legs are made, take the 16 stitches of the first leg and divide them between two needles – 8 stitches front, 8 stitches back. Repeat for the second leg. Knit across the front 8 stitches of one leg, cast on 3 stitches using backward loop cast on (this creates a space between the legs to make it easier to sew them up later), then knit across the front 8 stitches of second leg.

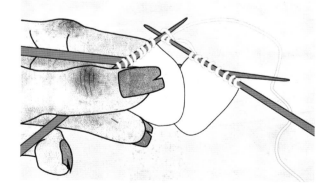

Working across the back of the second leg, knit 8 stitches, then cast on 3 stitches using the backward loop method. Knit the remaining 8 stitches on the first leg. You now have two needles with 18 stitches on each. Divide the stitches between 3 needles and continue to knit in the round.

1. *K4, k2tog* 4 times, k2 (32 st).
2. Knit 4 rounds.

The needles must now be repositioned so that the rows begin at centre back. To do this, slip the first 8 stitches onto a new needle, then the next 8 stitches onto another needle. The remaining stitches should go onto a third needle. Break the yarn and rejoin at the second set of 8 stitches to begin knitting in the round.

3. Kfb, k3, kfb, k3, kfb, k14, kfb, k3, kfb, k3, kfb (38 st).
4. Knit 1 round.
5. Kfb, k4, kfb, k4, kfb, k16, kfb, k4, kfb, k4, kfb (44 st).
6. Knit 1 round.
7. Kfb, k5, kfb, k5, kfb, k18, kfb, k5, kfb, k5, kfb (50 st).
8. Knit 1 round.
9. Kfb, k6, kfb, k6, kfb, k20, kfb, k6, kfb, k6, kfb (56 st).
10. Knit 1 round.
11. Kfb, k7, kfb, k7, kfb, k22, kfb, k7, kfb, k7, kfb (62 st).
12. Knit 1 round.
13. Kfb, k8, kfb, k8, kfb, k24, kfb, k8, kfb, k8, kfb (68 st).
14. Knit 1 round.
15. Kfb, k9, kfb, k9, kfb, k26, kfb, k9, kfb, k9, kfb (74 st).
16. Knit 1 round.
17. Kfb, K5, kfb, k10, kfb, k28, kfb, k10, kfb, k10, kfb (80 st).
18. Knit 1 round.
19. Kfb, K11, kfb, k11, kfb, k30, kfb, k11, kfb, k11, kfb (86 st).
20. Knit 10 rounds.
21. Stuff the remainder of the legs and the body/head.
22. K2tog, k11, k2tog, k11, k2tog, k30, k2tog, k11, k2tog, k11, k2tog (80 st).
23. Knit 1 round.
24. K2tog around (40 st).
25. Knit 1 round.
26. K2tog around (20 st).
27. Position and affix the safety eyes.
28. Knit 1 round.
29. K2tog around (10 st).
30. Knit 1 round.
31. Cut yarn, leaving a long tail. Thread a tapestry needle and run it through the remaining stitches. Top up the head with stuffing before pulling firmly closed.

Arms (make 2)

Cast on 5 stitches in ecru DK and divide for knitting in the round.

1. Knit 1 round.
2. Kfb in every stitch (10 st).
3. Knit 1 round.
4. Kfb in every stitch (20 st).
5. Knit 1 round.
6. K1, kfb around (30 st).
7. Work fur stitch for 2 repeats.
8. K3, k2tog around (24 st).
9. Work 2nd, 3rd and 4th rows of fur stitch.
10. K2, k2tog around (18 st).
11. Work 2nd, 3rd and 4th rows of fur stitch.
12. K1, k2tog around (12 st).
13. Work 2nd, 3rd and 4th rows of fur stitch.
14. Work fur stitch for 11 repeats.
15. Knit 3 rounds in stockinette stitch.
16. Cast off.

To assemble:

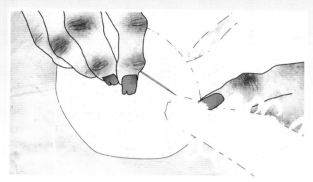

Step 1 Stuff the hands lightly and sew the arms to the body.

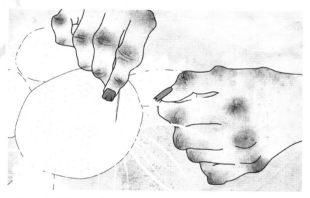

Step 3 Using mohair yarn, knot lengths of thread randomly all over head to make wispy hair. Trim to length, leaving some long pieces.

Step 2 Cut out a piece of black felt for the mouth. Use six to eight white tooth-shaped beads for teeth – position them in the mouth and sew in place. Alternatively, use white yarn to embroider teeth onto the black felt. Attach the felt patch to the face and sew firmly in place with black cotton thread.

Kraken Tentacle

'Below the thunders of the upper deep;

Far, far beneath in the abysmal sea,

His ancient, dreamless, uninvaded sleep

The Kraken sleepeth...'
Lord Alfred Tennyson, *The Kraken* (1830)

Legends of a colossal sea monster, dwelling deep in the cold northern oceans, date back to the time of the ancient Greeks. The poet Homer told of a six-headed monster named Scylla and Viking Sagas warned against mistaking the sleeping creature for an island. Whispered tales of ships capsized by errant tentacles, or sucked down into the maelstrom of this gargantuan creature's wake have struck fear into the hearts of even the most intrepid sailors. Reports continued into the eighteenth century, and the Kraken even found its way into Carolus Linneas' landmark scientific work *Systema Naturae* in 1735 (though it was removed in subsequent editions). Giant squid have been known to attack modern ships in deep waters, so who knows what monstrous beasts really linger beneath the waves?

This huge severed tentacle makes a great draft excluder or an interesting throw pillow. Or you could curl it up and make a comfy kitty bed for your unwitting furry friend.

Note:

This project uses so much I-cord, that the use of a Clover Wonder Knitter is recommended. Not only is it fun to use, but the chunky yarn combined with the 6-pin wheel makes the perfect size of I-cord for this project. If you would rather make your I-cord in the traditional manner, you can use 7.5mm (size 10/11) dpns instead.

You will need:

- ☠ 5mm (size 8) double-pointed needles (dpns)
- ☠ 7.5mm (size 10/11) double-pointed needles (dpns) (optional)
- ☠ Adriafil Navy Cotton Chunky yarn: 6 balls green (67) and 3 balls orange (53)
- ☠ Plastic canvas
- ☠ Clover Wonder Knitter
- ☠ Tapestry needle

Tentacle:

1. On 5mm (size 8) dpns, cast on 9 stitches in green. Place marker.
2. Knit 1 round.
3. Kfb in every stitch (18 st).
4. Knit 3 rounds.
5. Kfb in every stitch (36 st).
6. Knit 4 rounds.
7. Kfb in every stitch (72 st).
8. Knit 5 rounds.

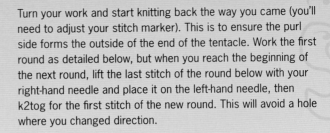

Turn your work and start knitting back the way you came (you'll need to adjust your stitch marker). This is to ensure the purl side forms the outside of the end of the tentacle. Work the first round as detailed below, but when you reach the beginning of the next round, lift the last stitch of the round below with your right-hand needle and place it on the left-hand needle, then k2tog for the first stitch of the new round. This will avoid a hole where you changed direction.

9. Knit 24, purl 24, knit 24 for 3 rounds.
10. K2tog, k22, p2tog, p22, k2tog, k22 (69 st).
11. Knit 23, purl 23, knit 23 for 8 rounds.
12. K2tog, k21, p2tog, p21, k2tog, k21 (66 st).
13. Knit 22, purl 22, knit 22 for 8 rounds.
14. K2tog, k20, p2tog, P20, k2tog, k20 (63 st).
15. Knit 21, purl 21, knit 21 for 8 rounds.
16. K2tog, k19, p2tog, p19, k2tog, k19 (60 st).
17. Knit 20, purl 20, knit 20 for 8 rounds.
18. K2tog, k18, p2tog, p18, k2tog, k18 (57 st).
19. Knit 19, purl 19, knit 19 for 8 rounds.
20. K2tog, k17, p2tog, p17, k2tog, k17 (54 st).
21. Knit 18, purl 18, knit 18 for 16 rounds.
22. K2tog, k16, p2tog, p16, k2tog, k16 (51 st).
23. Knit 17, purl 17, knit 17 for 16 rounds.

Place stitches on stitch holders or a long circular needle and turn work inside out. Cut a 14.5cm (5¾in) diameter circle of plastic canvas and secure it to the round end of the tentacle by sewing around the edge of the canvas. Add a few stitches in the centre to hold it in place. Weave in yarn ends and turn work right-side out. Carefully stuff the tentacle, making sure that it isn't overfilled or lumpy.

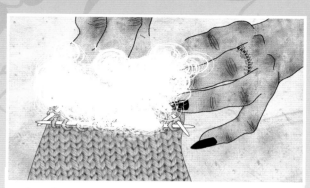

From here onwards, stuff the tentacle as you go until you reach the end.

24. K2tog, k15, p2tog, p15, k2tog, k15 (48 st).
25. Knit 16, purl 16, knit 16 for 16 rounds.
26. K2tog, k14, p2tog, p14, k2tog, k14 (45 st).
27. Knit 15, purl 15, knit 15 for 16 rounds.
28. K2tog, k13, p2tog, p13, k2tog, k13 (42 st).
29. Knit 14, purl 14, knit 14 for 40 rounds.
30. K2tog, k12, p2tog, p12, k2tog, k12 (39 st).
31. Knit 13, purl 13, knit 13 for 30 rounds.
32. K2tog, k11, p2tog, p11, k2tog, k11 (36 st).
33. Knit 12, purl 12, knit 12 for 8 rounds.
34. K2tog, k10, p2tog, p10, k2tog, k10 (33 st).
35. Knit 11, purl 11, knit 11 for 8 rounds.
36. K2tog, k9, p2tog, p9, k2tog, k9 (30 st).
37. Knit 10, purl 10, knit 10 for 8 rounds.
38. K2tog, k8, p2tog, p8, k2tog, k8 (27 st).
39. Knit 9, purl 9, knit 9 for 8 rounds.
40. K2tog, k7, p2tog, p7, k2tog, k7 (24 st).
41. Knit 8, purl 8, knit 8 for 8 rounds.
42. K2tog, k6, p2tog, p6, k2tog, k6 (21 st).
43. Knit 7, purl 7, knit 7 for 8 rounds.
44. K2tog, k5, p2tog, p5, k2tog k5 (18 st).
45. Knit 6, purl 6, knit 6 for 8 rounds.
46. K2tog, K4, p2tog, p4, k2tog, k4 (15 st).
47. Knit 5, purl 5, knit 5 for 4 rounds.
48. K2tog, k3, p2tog, p3, k2tog, k3 (12 st).
49. Knit 4, purl 4, knit 4 for 4 rounds.
50. K2tog, k2, p2tog, p2, k2tog, k2 (9 st).
51. Knit 3, purl 3, knit 3 for 1 row.
52. K2tog, k1, p2tog, p1, k2tog, k1 (6 st).
53. Cut yarn and thread through remaining stitches. Pull to close.

Suckers:

With the Clover Wonder Knitter and the 6-pin wheel (or 7.5mm [size 10/11] dpns and 6 stitches) work the following lengths of I-cord:

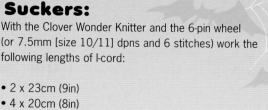

- 2 x 23cm (9in)
- 4 x 20cm (8in)
- 4 x 18cm (7in)
- 6 x 16cm (6¼in)
- 4 x 14cm (5½in)
- 8 x 12cm (4¾in)

Change to the 3-pin wheel (or 3 stitches on 7.5mm [size 10/11]) and work four 10cm (4in) lengths.

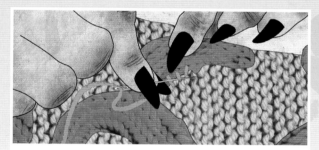

Sew all the pieces into loops and pin into place on the purl section of the tentacle in pairs. Sew in position.

Nosferatu

Forget slick hair and chiselled features, dress sense, charism, and sex appeal – vampires haven't always been the glamorous, sophisticated creatures they are today. Long before Bela Lugosi, Ann Rice and HBO made the undead attractive, a truly terrifying incarnation of the *vampyr* gave silent film-goers the fright of their lives. The hideous image of Count Orlok's long-fingered shadow creeping up the stairs in *Nosferatu* (1922) was an iconic moment in film history. Bringing plague and disease wherever he went, his spindly frame struck terror into the hearts of all who gazed upon him.

Nosferatu was the earliest (and unauthorized) adaptation of Bram Stoker's *Dracula*, whose estate sued for copyright infringement and won. The brilliantly chilling images of Count Orlok only survived because a single copy of the film escaped destruction. Since then, the count's grotesque hunch and shudder-worthy shadow have haunted nightmares for nearly a century.

This Nosferatu-inspired knitted character takes the fear to a new dimension with glowing yellow eyes. If you don't want to make the soft circuit, you can use small black safety eyes instead.

Note:

If you want to make these as hanging Halloween decorations, you can omit the pressure switch and just fit the battery in place so the eyes light up constantly. If you do this, it's best to leave a gap at the top when sewing around the battery. That way, you can easily slip the battery out to replace it (as it will run out much sooner!).

You will need:

- ☠ 3.25mm (size 3) double-pointed needles (dpns)
- ☠ DK yarn in lilac and black
- ☠ 2 x 5mm diffused LEDs in orange or yellow
- ☠ 1 x CR2032 lithium cell battery
- ☠ Round or needle nose pliers
- ☠ Conductive sewing thread
- ☠ Conductive fabric (optional)
- ☠ Felt scraps in black, white and red
- ☠ Cotton sewing thread and needle
- ☠ Fabric stiffener or PVA glue
- ☠ Copydex or fabric glue

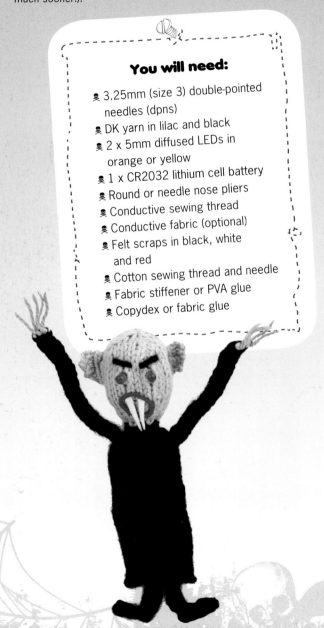

Body/head:

1. In black, cast on 18 st and divide for knitting in the round.
2. Work 25 rows in stocking stitch.
3. K2tog around (9 st).
4. *K1, k2tog* around (6 st).
5. Change to lilac yarn and *kfb* around (12 st).
6. *K1, kfb* around (18 st).
7. Work 3 rounds in stocking stitch.
8. *K2, kfb* around (24 st).
9. Work 7 rounds in stocking stitch.
10. *K4, k2tog* around (20 st).
11. *K3, k2tog* around (16 st).
12. *K2, k2tog* around (12 st).
13. Place stitches on stitch holder.

Soft circuit:

Cut out two pieces of black felt – one 10 x 3cm (4 x 1¼in) and one 4 x 3cm (1½ x 1¼in). Cut two square notches in the larger piece to make a 1cm (⅜in) (wide section in the middle. This is to ensure the felt fits through the neck opening.

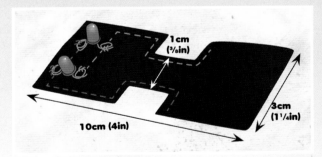

Twist the LEDs into shape with pliers (see page 28). Position the LED eyes in place on the felt patch, making sure that both positive loops are positioned toward the top of the patch. Thread a needle with 40cm (15¾in) of conductive thread, knot and carefully sew the positive ends of the LEDs to the patch. Continue to sew a running stitch down the side of the patch and through the narrow neck.

Cut another 40cm (15¾in) length of conductive thread and re-thread the needle. Work as before, sewing the negative loops of the LEDs to the felt patch. You can test your circuit at this point by holding the loose ends of the thread against the positive and negative sides of your battery.

Carefully pull the felt patch through the neck opening so that the LED part of the patch is inside the head and the other part is in the body. Make sure the felt running through the neck isn't folded over, to prevent the positive and negative threads coming into contact.

Make the soft circuit switch (see page 28) and fit the battery. Place the head stitches back on the needles. Push the LED eyes through from the inside of the head so they are sticking out. Stuff the head carefully, keeping the eyes in place.

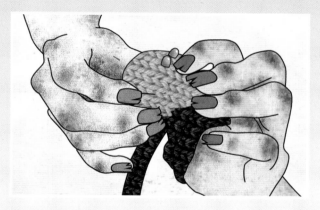

To finish the head:
14. *K1, k2tog* around (8 st).
15. Cut yarn, thread onto tapestry needle and run through remaining stitches. Pull to close.

Arms (make 2):
1. On 3.25mm (size 3) dpns, cast on 4 stitches in black yarn and work 7cm (2¾in) of I-cord.
2. Cast off and attach to body.

Legs (make 2):
On 3.25mm (size 3) dpns, cast on 5 stitches in black yarn and work 8cm (3in) of I-cord. Cast off. To make a foot, fold 1.5cm (⅝in) of the leg back on itself and secure it in place with a few stitches. Repeat the same process, making a foot for the second leg.

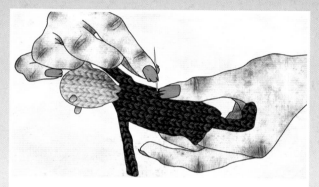

Push the legs you have just made up inside the body and sew them into place. Try to ensure that the feet point outwards.

Once the legs are in place, use a small amount of stuffing to fill the body cavity, making sure to pad the front and back of the soft circuit switch.

Ears:

On 3.25mm (size 3) needles, cast on 3 stitches in lilac.

Right ear:
1. K2, kfb (4 st).
2. Pfb, p3 (5 st).
3. Cast off.

Left ear:
1. Kfb, k2 (4 st).
2. P3, pfb (5 st).
3. Cast off.

Sew the ears to sides of head and weave in yarn ends.

Fingers:

Using a tapestry needle, carefully sew five lengths of lilac yarn to the ends of the hands, knotting in place. Paint them with fabric stiffener or diluted PVA glue and leave to dry on baking parchment or another non-stick surface (such as a silicone baking sheet). When completely dry, trim the ends to make them pointy. The glue will take a while to dry, so make sure you set aside plenty of time for this step.

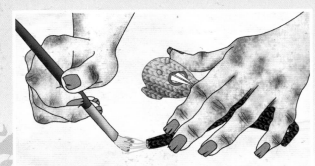

Mouth/teeth:

Cut an 'O' shape from a piece of red felt and glue it to the face. Carefully cut out two thin fangs from white felt, place on a non-stick surface and paint with fabric stiffener or diluted PVA glue. Leave to dry completely before gluing into place.

Eyebrows:

Using black yarn and a tapestry needle, sew two frowning eyebrows just above the eyes.

Grue Wallet

'The grue is a sinister, lurking presence in the dark places of the earth. Its favourite diet is adventurers, but its insatiable appetite is tempered by its fear of light. No grue has ever been seen by the light of day, and few have survived its fearsome jaws to tell the tale.' (Zork)

Every adventurer worth his Elvish sword knows better than to blunder wildly into a pitch-black room. After all, you are likely to be eaten by a grue. 'Horrible gurgling noises' and 'slavering fangs' await the adventurer foolish enough to have forgotten his Phial of Galadriel, so light a torch and set yourself to work on this fearsome grue wallet – guaranteed to keep your treasures safe from wandering chancers.

If you don't want to use a soft circuit, you can replace the 3mm LEDs with red glass beads. Likewise, you don't have to put in a zip if you don't want to – you could use more hook-and-loop tape or a button. You could even use an extra felt flap to make a credit card holder.

You will need:

- ☠ 3.75mm (size 5) knitting needles
- ☠ DK yarn in brown, black, grey and red
- ☠ Red and white felt
- ☠ Copydex or fabric glue
- ☠ 10cm (4in) brown, closed-end zip
- ☠ Sewing needle and brown and white thread
- ☠ Extra stiff 7-count plastic canvas
- ☠ 2 x 3mm red diffused LEDs
- ☠ Round or needle-nose pliers
- ☠ 1 x CR2032 coin cell battery
- ☠ Conductive thread
- ☠ Conductive fabric (optional)
- ☠ 10cm (4in) length of hook-and-loop tape
- ☠ 10cm (4in) Prym press-snap fasteners OR sew-on metal snap
- ☠ The chart from page 124

Cut a piece of red felt, 10.5 x 16cm (4¼ x 6¼in), and spread it with a thin layer of fabric glue or Copydex, leaving ⅜in (1cm) at each of the short ends. Position the felt in place on the reverse of the back red panel section, fold the piece in half and lightly weigh it down to help the glue to set evenly.

When dry, seam up the top and bottom edges of the felt-lined part of the wallet to make a pouch. Trim the felt if necessary, so that it lies flush with the knitted edges, and then carefully sew the zip into place. Seam up the top and bottom edges of the front door section.

Main body of wallet:

1. Cast on 25 stitches in grey yarn.
2. Work the pattern from the chart as illustrated (see page 124), making sure to knit (not purl) rows 26 and 78 to make a ridge on the right-hand side of the work.
3. At row 52, work 6 rows in garter stitch (knit, purl, knit, purl, knit, purl) to make the spine of the wallet. Then recommence working the chart from row 53 to 79.
4. After working the chart, change to red yarn and work 25 rows in stocking stitch. Cast off and weave in all ends.

Blocking the piece will make it easier to work with – see page 21 for more details. Next, take half of your metal snap and fix or sew it into place on the red section of the wallet.

Soft circuit:

Cut out two pieces of black felt – one 7 x 3cm (2¾ x 1¼in) and one 3 x 3cm (1¼ x 1¼in). The smaller piece is used for the pressure switch, while the larger is the main circuit patch.

Twist the LEDs into shape with pliers (see page 28). Position the LED eyes in place on the larger felt patch, making sure that both positive loops are positioned towards the top of the patch. Thread a needle with 30cm (12in) of conductive thread, knot, and carefully sew the positive ends of the LEDs to the patch. Continue sewing a running stitch down the side of the patch.

Cut another 30cm (12in) length of conductive thread and thread the needle. Sew the negative loops of the LEDs to the felt patch, continuing down the opposite side. Test your circuit by holding the ends of the thread against your battery.

Make the pressure switch at the base of your felt patch (see page 29). Fit the battery and sew closed.

To assemble:

Cut a piece of plastic canvas measuring 7 x 11cm (2¾ x 4½in) and trim the corners to prevent them from poking through the wallet. Slip the plastic canvas into the door pouch of the wallet. Take your soft circuit patch and position it inside the pouch so that the LED eyes poke out through the bars of the door. Holding the patch and canvas together firmly, remove from the pouch and sew the circuit patch firmly to the plastic canvas. If you are using a Prym snap, cut a 1.5cm (⅝in) square, 5mm (⅜in) from the edge of the plastic canvas to allow the two pieces of the snap to connect through the knitted fabric.

Trim the hook-and-loop tape to a width of 1cm (⅜in) and trim to length. Pin to the opening of the front pouch and sew in place.

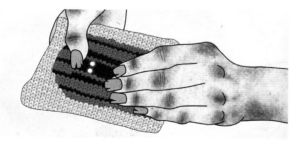

Slip the plastic canvas and soft circuit back into the pouch, poke the LED eyes through to the front of the work, and close the pouch with the hook-and-loop tape. If using a Prym snap, fix this in place through the hole you cut in the plastic canvas.

Teeth:

Using sharp scissors, cut four long fang shapes and six shorter fang shapes from white felt. Carefully spread the backs of each piece of felt with glue and press them into place on the red part of the wallet. When the glue is completely dry, carefully sew around the edge of each tooth using appliqué blanket stitch.

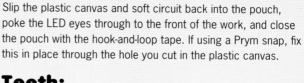

Zombie Marionette

*'Every dead body that is not exterminated becomes one of them.
It gets up and kills! The people it kills get up and kill!'*
Dawn of the Dead (1978)

Numbering a potential seven billion, zombies are our neighbours, our friends and our family; they are everyone we meet in the street. They may be slow and uncoordinated, but their sheer numbers make them an overwhelming force. Where you see one, you can be certain that many more are not far behind. Remember, always kill any contaminated members of your group, or they'll only end up murderously lumbering after you later.

The parts of this string puppet are mainly knitted in the round on double-pointed needles. The legs and arms are stiffened with dowelling rods and the feet are weighted with pennies or curtain weights. To make the dungarees, use any DK cotton or other yarn with a good drape.

As a finishing touch, embroider on some gore using French knots and chain stitch. You can really go to town here – use acrylic paint to make bloodstains and splashes, pipe cleaners for jutting-out bones and add holes and pulled threads to clothes to give a suitably dishevelled look.

You will need:

- ☠ 3.5mm (size 4) double-pointed needles (dpns)
- ☠ 4mm (size 6) knitting needles
- ☠ Double knitting (DK) yarn in grey, black and red
- ☠ DK cotton yarn in denim blue (Rowan Denim cotton in Tennessee was used here)
- ☠ Polyester fibre toy stuffing
- ☠ Thin wooden dowelling
- ☠ 2 x 8mm (⁵⁄₁₆in) black plastic safety eyes
- ☠ 6 x 10mm (³⁄₈in) metal jump rings
- ☠ Tapestry needle
- ☠ 2 x small, 1cm (³⁄₈in) buttons for dungarees
- ☠ Strong black cotton thread
- ☠ Red felt for mouth
- ☠ Plastic canvas or card for shoe soles
- ☠ 2 x pennies or curtain weights for shoes
- ☠ 3 x 15cm (6in) lengths of thick wooden dowelling or flat narrow wood (about the width of a ruler) – these are the support rods for the marionette
- ☠ 1 x 30cm (12in) length of flat narrow wood
- ☠ Strong black thread or yarn (Twilleys Goldfingering in Jet Black was used here)
- ☠ Fabric glue or Copydex
- ☠ Hairspray (optional)
- ☠ Corrugated cardboard

Body:

1. On 3.5mm (size 4) dpns, cast on 4 stitches in grey yarn.
2. Kfb to end (8 st)
3. Divide on 3 needles, kfb to end (16 st). Join to work in the round.
4. K1, * kfb, k2* repeat 2 times, kfb, k1 * kfb, k2* repeat 2 times, kfb (22 st).
5. K1, * kfb, k3* repeat 2 times, kfb, k2 * kfb, k3* repeat 2 times, kfb, k1 (28 st).
6. Knit 28 rounds straight.
7. Divide between two needles, stuff and graft (see page 20).

Head:

1. On 3.5mm (size 4) dpns, cast on 3 stitches in grey.
2. Kfb to end (6 stitches).
3. Divide onto 3 needles, *kfb, k1* repeat to end (9 st). Join to work in the round.
4. *K1, kfb, k1* repeat to end (12 st).
5. *K3, kfb * repeat to end (15 st).
6. *K4, kfb * repeat to end (18 st).
7. *K5, kfb * repeat to end (21 st).
8. Knit 9 rounds straight.
9. *K5, k2tog* repeat to end (18 st).
10. *K4, k2tog* repeat to end (15 st).
11. With stitches still on the needles, turn the head inside out and affix the safety eyes. Turn right-side out and stuff head with polyester fibre toy filling.
12. K1, then *k2tog* repeat to end (8 st).
13. Knit 3 rounds for neck, cast off.
14. Stuff the neck firmly and sew the head to the top edge of the body (the cast-on edge), at a slight angle. Cut a yawning 'O'-shaped mouth from red felt and glue into place.

Hair:

Cut out a 6 x 10cm (2½ x 4in) piece of corrugated cardboard. Fold in half lengthways to make a double thickness card measuring 3 x 5cm (1¼ x 2in). Using black yarn and starting at one end, wrap the yarn around the card, single thickness, until you reach the end. Cut the yarn and hold in place.

Using a sewing needle and thread, sew across the top of the wrapped yarn to hold the strands together. It's best to go back and forth a few times to ensure it's secure. Carefully slide the yarn off the cardboard and cut through the bottom loops to make your wig. Sew the wig onto the top of the head – you can use fabric glue to secure some of the lower strands to the back and sides of the head. If you have any bald patches, take a needle threaded with a length of black yarn and fill them in with long stitches. Cut and style your hair – you can use a light spray of hairspray to finish.

Legs (make 2):

1. On 4 (3.5mm) dpns, cast on 3 stitches in grey.
2. Kfb in every stitch (6 st).
3. Divide between 3 needles.
4. Working in the round, *k1, kfb* repeat to end (9 st).
5. Knit until work measures 15cm (6in).
6. K1 then *k2tog* repeat around (5 st).
7. Run thread through, but leave very loose.

For each leg, cut two 7cm (2¾in) lengths of dowelling. Insert a length of dowelling through the open end of the knitted leg and push down to the ankle (closed) end. Using grey yarn, sew across the knee to enclose the dowelling in the leg. Then insert a second length of dowelling to make the top part of the leg. Pull the cast-off yarn firmly to close and sew a jump ring in place to make the hip joint. Repeat this process to make the second leg. Sew the legs to the body using the jump ring as the join.

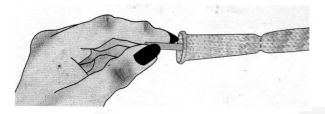

Arms (make 2):

1. On 3.5mm (size 4) dpns, cast on 3 stitches in grey.
2. Kfb in every stitch (6 st).
3. Divide between 3 needles.
4. Working in the round, *k1, kfb* repeat to end (9 st).
5. Knit until work measures 9cm (3½in).
6. Run thread through, but leave very loose.

For each arm, cut a 8.5cm (3⅜in) length of dowelling and insert into the open end of the knitted arm, pushing down to the wrist (closed end). Pull the cast-off yarn tightly to close and sew a jump ring in place for the shoulder joint. Repeat this for the second arm. Sew the arms to the body using the jump rings as the joins.

Hands (make 2):

1. On 3.5mm (size 4) dpns, cast on 3 stitches in grey.
2. Kfb in every stitch (6 st).
3. Divide on 3 needles.
4. Working in the round, *k1, kfb* repeat to end (9 st).
5. Knit until work measures 4cm (1½in).
6. K2tog once, divide on 2 needles (4 st each side).
7. Stuff lightly and graft using Kitchener stitch.

Take a 10mm (⅜in) metal jump ring and sew it to the wrist end of the arm with grey yarn. Then sew one of the hands to the same jump ring – the cast-on edge of the hand is the wrist end. Repeat this for the second arm and hand.

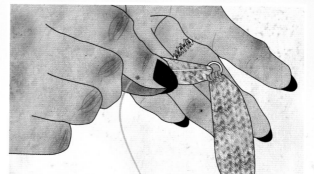

Dungarees:

1. On 4mm (size 6) needles, cast on 20 stitches in denim blue for bottom of the trouser leg.
2. Purl 1 row.
3. Knit 1 row.
4. Purl 1 row.
5. Beginning knit row, work 36 rows in stocking stitch
6. Cast off 2 stitches at beginning of next 2 rows (16 st)
7. Place on stitch holder and repeat rows 1–6 to make the second trouser leg.
8. With the second trouser leg still on the needles, knit 1 row then knit across first leg from stitch holder to join the two pieces together (32 st).
9. Work 8 rows in stocking stitch.
10. Work 11 stitches knit, 10 purl, 11 knit.
11. Work 11 stitches purl, 10 knit, 11 purl.
12. Cast off 9 stitches at beginning of next 2 rows (14 st).
13. Work 2 stitches knit, 10 purl, 2 knit.
14. Knit 14.
15. Repeat rows 13 and 14 twice to make dungarees bib.
16. Repeat row 13.
17. Knit 1 row.
18. Purl 1 row.
19. Cast off.

Block carefully to prevent the edges curling (see page 21). Fold each trouser leg in half lengthwise and seam up the inner leg using mattress stitch. Fold the waist piece in half and seam. Carefully sew the crotch closed.

Dungaree straps:

1. On 3.5mm (size 4) needles, cast on 35 stitches in denim blue.
2. Knit 1 row.
3. Cast off 25 stitches, knit to end.
4. Knit 10 stitches, cast on 25.
5. Cast off.

Sew the long single strap to the centre back of the trousers. Now dress your zombie! Poke the legs into the holes and pull the straps of the dungarees up and over the shoulders – sew the straps onto the front bib of the dungarees with two small buttons.

Shoes (make 2):

1. On 3.5mm (size 4) needles, cast on 4 stitches in black yarn for the sole of shoe.
2. K1, kfb, kfb, k1 (6 st).
3. Work 15 rows in garter stitch.
4. K1, k2tog, k2tog, k1 (4 st).
5. Cast off.
6. On 3.5mm (size 4) needles, cast on 4 stitches in black for the top of the shoe.
7. K1, kfb, kfb, k1 (6 st).
8. Work 5 rows in stocking stitch.
9. K1, kfb, k2, kfb, k1 (8 st).
10. Work 5 rows in stocking stitch.
11. K2tog across (4 st).
12. Cast off.

Sew the three sides of the sole piece and the top piece together, making sure the knit side of the top piece is facing outwards. Cut a small piece of card or plastic canvas the same size as the sole. Sew or glue a penny or curtain weight onto this, then slot it inside the shoe and stuff. Sew closed. Repeat for second shoe. Firmly sew the shoes to the legs, with the ankle end of the leg attached to the top edge of the shoe.

Stringing your puppet:

Stringing requires an element of fine tuning to ensure the legs and arms hang properly. The threads should be cut longer than needed, then shortened accordingly as the puppet is strung. Cut two 60cm (24in) lengths of strong black thread. Using a tapestry needle, sew through the dungarees to the legs, just above the knees. Cut another two lengths of thread and sew to the shoulders, just underneath the dungaree straps.

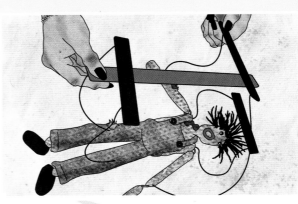

Don't sew the strings to the jump rings – they are there to help the limbs move freely. Cut two more lengths of thread and sew to the arms, just above the wrist jump rings.

Attach the shoulder strings to one of the 15cm (6in) wooden rods – you can either tie them on, or drill holes at either side and feed the strings through. Shorten the strings as you fix them, around 25–30cm (10–12in) from shoulders to rod is a good length. The weight of the body is supported by this rod.

Attach the arm threads to another 15cm (6in) rod. Adjust the string length so that when held together with the shoulder rod, the arms are very slightly raised.

Now attach the knee strings to the last 15cm (6in) rod. Adjust the string length so that the legs hang straight down, thread taut, when the rod is held together with the shoulder rod.

The final rod, 30cm (12in) in length, is used to manipulate the puppet. Balance the shoulder support rod over the top, then hook the leg and arm rods over. You can now work the leg and arm rods independently, while keeping them supported with the long rod.

Finishing touches:

Step 1 Every good zombie needs a neck wound! Use red DK yarn to embroider French knots and chain stitches onto the neck. Sew loops of grey yarn around the wound and snip through threads to fray the edges – be careful not to cut through any of your knitting.

Step 2 More wounds and bites can be made in the same way. You could also splash and splatter on some red paint and rub dirt into the knees. Make holes or slashes in the dungarees by sewing around your target area to prevent fraying, then snipping a few stitches inside. Rub gently with your fingers to loosen.

Creature from the Black Lagoon Sleep Mask

Slip on this terrifying mask and unless you are unlucky enough to be kidnapped by a gang of meddling scientists, it's pretty much guaranteed that you'll enjoy your forty winks free of disturbances. Alternatively, feel free to maul anyone who unwittingly wanders into your lair.

Although the black lagoon's creature hailed from Jack Arnold's 1954 monster flick, the movie's title has passed into general usage – most often referring to a teenage boy who emerges from his room after days of unwashed pizza-eating and video game-induced stupor, communicating only in grunts. Both versions are equally terrifying and likely to ward off intruders.

This mask is easy to customize, because the features are added afterwards in felt. If you don't want to use felt for the backing, you could knit a second mask piece in black instead – make sure to use a non-scratchy yarn if you decide to do this. Sleeping in a mouldy cavern and kidnapping meddling beauties is, of course, entirely optional.

10. Sl1p, k2tog, k14, k2tog, k1 (18 st).
11. Knit 9 rows.
12. Sl1p, k2tog, k15 (17 st).
13. Sl1p, k13, k2tog, k1 (16 st).
14. Sl1p, k2tog, k13 (15 st).
15. Sl1p, k11, k2tog, k1 (14 st).
16. Sl1p, k2tog, k11 (13 st).
17. Sl1p, k10, kfb, k1 (14 st).
18. Sl1p, kfb, k12 (15 st).
19. Sl1p, k12, kfb, k1 (16 st).
20. Sl1p, kfb, k14 (17 st).
21. Sl1p, k14, kfb, k1 (18 st).
22. Knit 9 rows.
23. Sl1p, kfb, k14, kfb, k1 (20 st).
24. Knit 9 rows.
25. Sl1p, kfb, k16, kfb, k1 (22 st).
26. Knit 10 rows.
27. Sl1p, k2tog, k16, k2tog, k1 (20 st).
28. Sl1p, k2tog, k14, k2tog, k1 (18 st).
29. Sl1p, k2tog, k12, k2tog, k1 (16 st).
30. Sl1p, k2tog, k10, k2tog, k1 (14 st).
31. Sl1p, k2tog, k8, k2tog, k1 (12 st).
32. Cast off loosely.

To assemble:

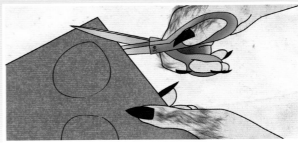

Step 1 Cut out two 3.5cm (1⅜in) diameter circles of red felt, two 2.5cm (1in) diameter circles of yellow felt and two 1.5cm (½in) circles of black felt. Cut across the top of each circle and then put them together, black on top of yellow, on top of red. Use glue to hold the circles in place, then a dab of glue to hold the eye patch in place on the mask. With red thread, sew around the felt patch using an appliqué stitch.

Mask:

1. On 3.25mm (size 3) needles, cast on 12 stitches in green.
2. Sl1p, kfb, k8, kfb, k1 (14 st).
3. Sl1p, kfb, k10, kfb, k1 (16 st).
4. Sl1p, kfb, k12, kfb, k1 (18 st).
5. Sl1p, kfb, k14, kfb, k1 (20 st).
6. Sl1p, kfb, k16, kfb, k1 (22 st).
7. Knit 10 rows.
8. Sl1p, k2tog, k16, k2tog, k1 (20 st).
9. Knit 9 rows.

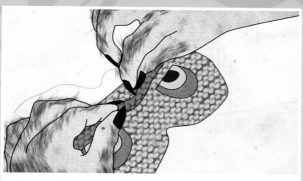

Step 2 Make an eyebrow by casting on 3 stitches on 3.25mm (size 3) dpns and knitting 16cm (6¼in) of icord. Sew this into place above the eyes, using the pictures as a guide.

Step 4 Cut a piece of elastic about 34–38cm (13½–15in) long (depending on the size of your head). With black thread, sew the black felt to the back of the eyemask, catching about 2cm (¾in) of elastic between the felt and the mask. Sew over the elastic several times to make sure it is firmly attached.

Step 3 Block the mask to shape it (see page 21). Once it's dry, draw carefully around the edge of the mask onto a piece of paper to make the template for the felt backing and cut this out. You can ensure this is symmetrical by folding it in half and trimming it so that both sides are exactly the same. When you're happy with the shape, draw around your template onto a piece of black felt using tailors' chalk or a fabric marker, and carefully cut this out.

Haunted House Diorama

Everyone loves a good haunted house. Stories of homes possessed by demons, poltergeists and malevolent spirits, walls that drip blood, and things that go bump in the night are a mainstay of literature that can be traced back hundreds of years. From the creaking corridors of *The Amityville Horror* (1979) to a generational curse in *Ju-On* (2003), the haunted house is an idea that strikes deep in the psyche of horror fans – the evil spirits seek you where you live. On average, a third of the population believe they have been in a haunted house, but few are as scary as this one.

Gravestones, skulls and a haunted tree enhance the property value of this creepy crib. You can choose from different shaped headstones to give that authentic horror-film look, and the gnarly tree's twisted limbs stand ready to snatch sleeping children from their beds. An alarming abode currently inhabited by a coven of witches, this house could be populated by ghosts, vampires or anything else that takes your fancy.

This knitted playhouse also opens up a world of possibilities for customization: experiment with different coloured walls, make a tiny rug for the floor or decorate the walls with spooky pictures.

You will need:

- ☠ 3.25mm (size 3) needles
- ☠ Double knitting (DK) yarn in light purple, dark purple, black, green, yellow, grey and brown (King Cole Bamboo DK was used here)
- ☠ Ultra stiff plastic canvas
- ☠ Yarn or tapestry needle
- ☠ Chart from page 125

Note

It's easy to get into a mess when working with intarsia – make sure to wind all of your yarn onto bobbins before you start knitting with it, or you'll find the tangles will make it hard to maintain an even tension and the finished patterns will appear distorted.

Tension: 34 rows and 24 stitches = 10cm (4in) square.

Front piece:

On 3.25mm (size 3) needles, cast on 30 stitches in light purple and follow the chart on page 125 for the front piece, beginning with a knit row. To make a neat selvage, knit the first stitch of every row, even on the purl side. All increases and decreases are worked one stitch in from the edge, as indicated on the chart.

Front inside piece:
Follow the chart for the front inside piece, remembering to knit your selvage.

Back piece:

To make the back piece of the house, follow the chart on page 125 for the front piece, omitting the door and the attic window. You could knit it in plain light purple if you wanted to.

Back inside piece:
The back inside piece is knitted in plain yellow. You can either work from one of the charts (ignoring the colour changes), or from the instructions below. This written pattern is also useful if you are struggling to get to grips with the shaping as shown on the chart.

1. On 3.25mm (size 3) needles, cast on 30 stitches in yellow yarn.
2. Beginning with a knit row, work 6 rows of stocking stitch. Remember to knit the first stitch of every row to maintain your selvage.
3. K1, kfb, k26, kfb, k1 (32 st).
4. Work 8 rows stocking stitch, ending knit row.
5. K1, pfb, p28 pfb, k1 (34 st).
6. Work 10 rows stocking stitch, ending purl row.
7. K1, kfb, k30, kfb, k1 (36 st).

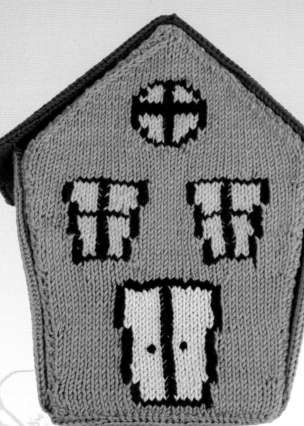

8. Work 7 rows stocking stitch, ending purl row.
9. K1, kfb, k32, kfb, k1 (38 st).
10. Work 9 rows stocking stitch, ending purl row.
11. K1, kfb, k34, kfb, k1 (40 st).
12. Work 8 rows, ending knit row.
13. K1, p2tog, p34, p2tog, k1 (38 st).
14. Knit 1 row.
15. K1, p2tog, p32, p2tog, k1 (36 st).
16. K1, k2tog, k30, k2tog, k1 (34 st).
17. K1, p2tog, p28, p2tog, k1 (32 st).
18. Knit 1 row.
19. K1, p2tog, p26, p2tog, k1 (30 st).
20. K1, k2tog, k24, k2tog, k1 (28 st).
21. K1, p26, k1.
22. K1, k2tog, k22, k2tog, k1 (26 st).
23. K1, p2tog, p20, p2tog, k1 (24 st).
24. Knit 1 row.
25. K1, p2tog, p18, p2tog, k1 (22 st).
26. K1, k2tog, k16, k2tog, k1 (20 st).
27. K1, p18, k1.
28. K1, k2tog, k14, k2tog, k1 (18 st).
29. K1, p2tog, p12, p2tog, k1 (16 st).
30. K1, k2tog, k10, k2tog, k1 (14 st).
31. K1, p2tog, p8, p2tog, k1 (12 st).
32. K1, k2tog, k6, k2tog, k1 (10 st).
33. K1, p2tog, p4, p2tog, k1 (8 st).
34. K1, k2tog, k2, k2tog, k1 (6 st).
35. K1, p2tog, p2tog, k1 (4 st).
36. K2tog, k2tog (2 st).
37. K2tog (1 st).
38. Cut yarn and thread through remaining stitch, pull to close.

Carefully pin and block (see page 21) the four wall pieces to shape, following the measurements as shown on the right.

Cut two pieces of plastic canvas to the same dimensions. Take the front piece and the front inside piece and sew them together, right sides out, with the plastic canvas in-between. Do the same with the back piece and the back inside piece.

Side piece:

1. On 3.25mm (size 3) needles, cast on 38 stitches in light purple.
2. Work 139 rows in stocking stitch.

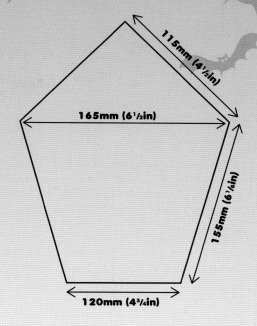

3. Cast off.
4. Fold piece in half lengthways and sew up seam using mattress stitch, leaving top and bottom open.

Cut out two pieces of 80mm (3¼in) x 153mm (6in) plastic canvas and one piece of 80mm (3¼in) x 120mm (4¾in) plastic canvas. Insert these into the side piece – the shorter canvas piece should be in the middle. Using light purple yarn, sew a line of stitches between each piece of canvas to keep them separate. Sew up the two open edges.

Roof:

1. On 3.25mm (size 3) needles, cast on 46 stitches in dark purple.
2. Work 88 rows in stocking stitch.
3. Cast off.
4. Fold piece in half lengthways and sew up the seam leaving the top and bottom open.

Cut out two pieces of 140mm (5½in) x 95mm (3¾in) plastic canvas and insert these into the knitted roof piece. Using dark purple yarn, sew a line of stitches between the two pieces of canvas to keep them separate. Sew up the two open edges.

Attic floor:

1. On 3.25mm (size 3) needles, cast on 37 stitches in brown. Work in stocking stitch throughout.
2. Work 5 rows brown.
3. Change to black, work 1 row.
4. Repeat rows 2 and 3 seven times (48 rows total).
5. Work 5 rows brown.
6. Cast off.

Fold the piece in half widthways and sew up the seam using mattress stitch, leaving the sides open. Cut a piece of plastic canvas 155mm (6⅛in) x 80mm (3¼in) and insert this into the knitted attic floor piece. Sew up the two open sides.

To assemble:

Step 1 First, tack the side piece to the back piece, and then sew firmly in place. Not all of your stitches need to go through the plastic canvas, but you should sew through the canvas at each corner to keep the structure as stable as possible. Keep your stitches small and neat.

Step 2 Take the front piece and sew the bottom edge firmly to the bottom edge of the back/side piece – this should form a 'hinge' that allows the front flap to fold outwards. Loosely tack the front piece to the sides at the top using large stitches – this will help keep the roof supported while you sew it in place.

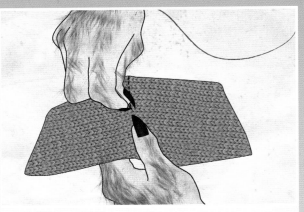

Step 3 Take your attic floor piece and position it so that it supports the side walls, but doesn't cause them to bulge out. Sew it to the sides of the house first and then sew along the back to secure.

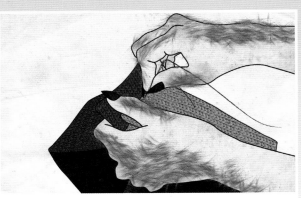

Step 4 First, tack the roof in place on top of the house, then sew first to the back, then to the sides. The roof should jut out slightly over the front of the house – this should stop the front flap from flopping open when the house is closed up. Remember not to sew the roof to the front piece of the house! Remove the tacking stitches and the front should be able to open and close.

Finishing touches:

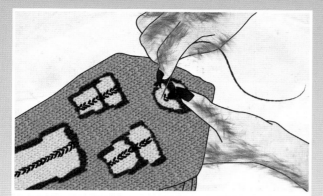

Using black yarn, embroider a central vertical line onto each of the windows and up the centre of the door using duplicate stitch (see page 26). Embroider two black handles on the door using French knots (see page 26).

Pile O' Skulls

These little skulls knit up super fast, so in no time at all you can have a pile big enough to rival the catacombs of Paris. As well as using them to adorn your haunted house diorama, they would make great earrings! You could also use them to decorate your Monster Merry-Go-Round (see page 70); hang them around the canopy or from different length threads on the frame.

To finish:

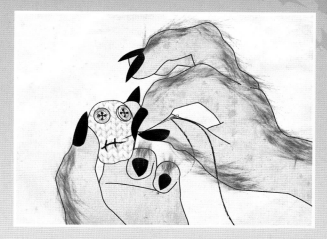

Starting at the cast-on edge, carefully seam up the back, stuffing firmly as you go. Weave in all ends and then sew on the buttons for eyes. With black embroidery thread, sew a long horizontal stitch for the mouth, then four or five shorter stitches over the top.

Skulls:

1. On 3.25mm (size 3) needles, cast on 4 stitches in white.
2. Kfb in every stitch (8 st).
3. Work 5 rows stocking stitch, ending purl row.
4. Kfb in every stitch (16 st).
5. Work 5 rows stocking stitch, ending purl row.
6. K2tog across (8 st).
7. P2tog across (4 st).
8. Cut yarn and thread through remaining stitches, pull to close.

Gravestones

No self-respecting haunted house would be seen dead without a few gravestones knocking about the grounds. There are two types of headstones to go with the haunted house diorama – one with a rectangular top and one curved.

You could also sew these little gravestones to a piece of felt or a knitted square to make place markers for a horror-themed dinner party. It's easy to make them a little bigger to suit your needs – just add a couple of extra stitches when casting on and a couple of extra rows when knitting. Stitch on initials with embroidery thread to identify your 'victims'.

You will need:

- ☠ 3.25mm (size 3) needles
- ☠ Double knitting (DK) yarn in grey and green
- ☠ Black fine yarn or embroidery thread and needle
- ☠ Polyester toy stuffing
- ☠ Card or plastic canvas

Curved gravestone (make 2):

1. On 3.25mm (size 3) needles, cast on 10 stitches in grey.
2. Work 12 rows stocking stitch, ending purl row.
3. K1, k2tog, k4, k2tog, k1 (8 st).
4. P1, p2tog, p2, p2tog, p1 (6 st).
5. K1, k2tog, k2tog, k1 (4 st).
6. Cut yarn and thread through remaining stitches.

Rectangular gravestone (make 2):

1. On 3.25mm (size 3) needles, cast on 10 stitches in grey.
2. Work 16 rows stocking stitch, ending purl row.
3. Cast off.

To assemble:

To assemble, seam the two pieces together, leaving the bottom end open. Cut two pieces of card or plastic canvas that will fit neatly inside, then make a thin sandwich by placing a small amount of polyester toy stuffing between them.

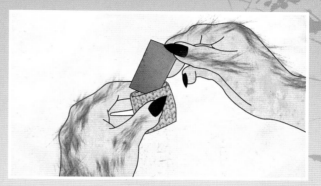

Carefully place the card/canvas pieces and stuffing inside your gravestone. Using black thread, stitch on a cross or initials to decorate, then carefully sew into place on your haunted house. Make sure the front flap of the house still closes when the gravestones are in position!

Finishing touches:

To make some tufts of grass around the base of your gravestone, sew loops of green yarn all around the base. You will need to secure each loop with stitches to prevent the tufts from pulling out. When you're done, take some sharp scissors and snip your grass to the desired length, ruffling with your fingers to fray the fibres.

Little Witches

'If she weighs the same as a duck…she's made of wood…and therefore…A WITCH!' Monty Python and the Holy Grail (1974)

Witches have had a rough time of it over the years, what with all the dunking and the burning. Harry Potter seems to have got away with it though. Can girls be wizards?

These little witches are weighted in the base with a small beanbag – you don't have to do this, but it does make them sit up nicely. All the better for dunking!

You will need:

- ☠ 3.25mm (size 3) needles
- ☠ 3.25mm (size 3) double-pointed needles (dpns)
- ☠ Double knitting (DK) yarn in green and black
- ☠ 2 x 7.5mm black safety eyes
- ☠ Polyester toy stuffing
- ☠ A pair of tights
- ☠ Lentils/dried beans
- ☠ Tapestry or yarn needle

Body/Head:

1. On 3.25mm (size 3) needles, cast on 3 stitches in black.
2. Purl 1 row.
3. Kfb across (6 st).
4. Purl 1 row.
5. Kfb across (12 st).
6. Purl 1 row.
7. Kfb across (24 st).
8. Purl 1 row.
9. Kfb across (48 st).
10. Work 5 rows stocking stitch, ending with a purl row.
11. K2tog across (24 st).
12. Work 7 rows stocking stitch, ending with a purl row.
13. K2tog across (12 st).
14. P2tog across (6 st).
15. Change to green, kfb across (12 st).
16. Purl 1 row.
17. Kfb across (24 st).
18. Work 9 rows stocking stitch, ending purl row.
19. K2tog across (12 st).
20. Purl 1 row.
21. K2tog across (6st).
22. Cut yarn and run thread through remaining stitches.

Beginning at the cast-on edge, seam halfway up the black section of the back. Make a small beanbag to weight the bottom by cutting the toe off a pair of old tights and filling it with a small amount of lentils, split peas or other small, dried beans. Sew the top of the beanbag closed and place the bag in the base of the witch.

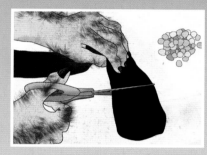

Fix the eyes in place at the front of the head. Continue to sew the seam closed, stuffing with polyester toy filling as you work.

Arms (make 2):

1. On 3.25mm (size 3) needles, cast on 2 stitches in black.
2. Kfb, kfb (4 st).
3. Pfb, p2, pfb (6 st).
4. Kfb, k4, kfb (8 st).
5. Work 3 rows stocking stitch (p, k, p).
6. Kfb across (16 st).
7. P2tog across (8 st).
8. K2tog across (4 st).
9. Cut yarn and run thread through the remaining stitches.

Lightly stuff and sew up seams. Sew to the sides of the body.

Hat:

1. On 3.25mm (size 3) dpns, cast on 30 stitches in black and divide on three needles for knitting in the round.
2. Knit 1 round.
3. Purl (to form a ridge).
4. Knit 1 round.
5. Purl 1 round.
6. *K3, k2tog* around (24 st).
7. Purl 1 round.
8. Knit 1 round.
9. *K2, k2tog* around (18 st).
10. Knit 3 rounds.
11. *K1, k2tog* around (12 st).
12. Knit 1 round.
13. K1, k2tog, k2, k2tog, k2, k2tog, k1 (9 st).
14. Knit 1 round.
15. *K1, k2tog* around (6 st).
16. Knit 1 round.
17. K2tog around, onto 1 needle (3 st).
18. Work 3 rows of I-cord.
19. K1, k2tog (2 st).
20. Work 1 row of I-cord.
21. K2tog (1 st).
22. Cut yarn, run through and tighten.

Sew the hat in position on the head.

Haunted Tree

Who could forget the creepy tree in *Poltergeist*, looming outside the bedroom window, ready to snatch the children from their beds? It's enough to make anyone shudder. No haunted house or graveyard would be complete without a twisted, gnarly tree, so grab your needles and let's get going!

You will need:

- ☠ 3.25mm (size 3) double-pointed needles (dpns)
- ☠ Double knitting (DK) yarn in brown tweed
- ☠ 2 x 15mm amber safety eyes
- ☠ 2 x pipe cleaners
- ☠ Brown felt
- ☠ Brown thread and sewing needle
- ☠ Fabric stiffener or PVA glue
- ☠ Polyester toy stuffing

Trunk:

1. On 3.25mm (size 3) dpns, cast on 39 stitches in brown and divide between three needles for knitting in the round.
2. Place stitch marker and knit 5 rounds.
3. *K11, k2tog* repeat (36 st).
4. Knit 3 rounds.
5. *K10, k2tog* repeat (33 st).
6. Knit 3 rounds.
7. *K9, k2tog* repeat (30 st).
8. Knit 3 rounds.
9. *K8, k2tog* repeat (27 st).
10. Knit 3 rounds.
11. *K7, k2tog* repeat (24 st).
12. Knit 3 rounds.
13. *K6, k2tog* repeat (21 st).
14. Knit 14 rounds.
15. Cast off.

The roots:

To form the roots of the tree, place a cylindrical item in the trunk, such as a cardboard tube, then 'pinch' the excess fabric at the base and stitch it together. Do this in three places. With your tube or cylinder still in place, cut a circle of brown felt to fit the base of your tree and sew in place with brown thread. Fix safety eyes onto front. Take a small dish or saucer with diluted PVA or neat fabric stiffener and dip the top of the tree into it, saturating the top 1cm (⅜in). Squeeze and work it into the fibres with your fingers and leave to dry completely. Stuff the trunk firmly, leaving 2.5cm (1in) of space at the top.

Arms (make 2):

1. On 3.25mm (size 3) dpns, cast on 12 stitches in brown.
2. Work 6 rows in stocking stitch, ending purl row.
3. K1, k2tog, k6, k2tog, k1 (10 st)
4. Work 6 rows stocking stitch, ending purl row.

5. K1, k2tog, k4, k2tog, k1 (8 st).
6. Work 3 rows stocking st (p, k, p).
7. K1, k2tog, k2, k2tog, k1 (6 st).
8. Work 13 rows stocking stitch, ending purl row.

Fingers:

9. Place back 4 stitches on stitch holder.
10. Using the remaining 2 stitches, work 6 rows in stocking stitch.
11. K2tog.
12. Knit 3 rows I-cord (1 stitch only).
13. Cast off.
14. Taking next 2 stitches from stitch holder, work 8 rows stocking stitch.
15. K2tog.
16. Knit 2 rows I-cord (1 st only).
17. Cast off.
18. On final 2 stitches from holder, work 6 rows stocking stitch.
19. K2tog.
20. Knit 3 rows I-cord (1 st only).
21. Cast off.

Seam up the branch, then carefully seam up each finger. Poke a pipe cleaner into the branch and trim so that none sticks out of the end, then fill the remaining space with polyester toy filling. Use a knitting needle to poke the stuffing in. Sew the branches firmly to the trunk of the tree.

To finish:

On 3.25mm (size 3) dpns, cast on 3 stitches and work two 3cm (1½in) lengths of I-cord to make the eyebrows, and one 6–7cm (2¼–2¾in) length to make the mouth. Sew the mouth and eyebrows to the trunk.

Using a pair of very sharp scissors, cut zigzags and snips into the top of the trunk – the fabric should feel quite stiff from the glue or stiffener you used.

When you're happy with the effect, dampen this glued area with a little water and rub gently with your fingers to fray and soften the cut edges.

Bend the branches of your tree to make them look more like arms. Dip the fingers in fabric stiffener or PVA glue and mould them into shape.

Cut another round piece of brown felt and stuff it into the top of the trunk to cover up the toy stuffing – you can also stuff the top with brown yarn off-cuts; leave a few hanging out for effect.

Intarsia Charts

Here, you will find all the charts you will need to complete the projects in the book, including the Creepy Clown Cushion Cover, page 66, the Grue Wallet, page 96 and the Haunted House, page 110. You may find it easier to enlarge the charts on a photocopier in order to use them. For more detailed instructions on using intarsia and colour charts for knitting, see page 23.

Creepy Clown Cushion Cover, page 66

☐ – pink
○ – white
⊘ – black
⊠ – blue
⊠ – red

Grue Wallet, page 96

⊞ – black
⊠ – brown
☐ – grey

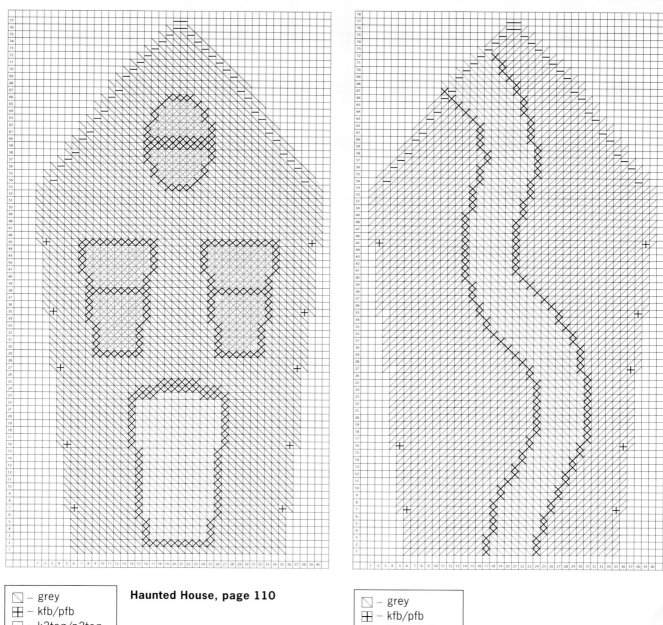

Haunted House, page 110

- ◻ – grey
- ⊞ – kfb/pfb
- ⊟ – k2tog/p2tog
- ◻ – light purple
- ⊠ – yellow
- ⊠ – black

- ◻ – grey
- ⊞ – kfb/pfb
- ⊟ – k2tog/p2tog
- ◻ – green
- ⊠ – black

Stitch Abbreviations

The abbreviations listed here are those you'll need to work the patterns for the projects in this book.

- **alt:** alternate
- **beg:** begin(ning)
- **cc:** contrasting colour
- **cm:** centimetre(s)
- **cont:** contin(e)(ing)
- **foll:** follow; follows; following
- **in:** inch(es)
- **inc:** increase(s)
- **k:** knit
- **k1p1 rib:** knit 1 stitch, purl 1 stitch – repeat as indicated in pattern
- **k2p2 rib:** knit 2 stitches, purl 2 stitches – repeat as indicated in pattern
- **k2tog:** knit the next 2 stitches together
- **kfb:** knit into front and back of next stitch
- **LH:** left hand
- **mc:** main colour
- **ml:** make loop

- **mm:** millimetre(s)
- **p:** purl
- **patt:** pattern
- **p2tog:** purl the next 2 stitches together
- **pfb:** purl into front and back of next stitch
- **rs or RS:** right side
- **s1, k1, psso:** slip next stitch, then knit one stitch and pass the slipped stitch over
- **s1, p1, psso:** slip next stitch, then purl one stitch and pass the slipped stitch over
- **sl1p:** slip next stitch purlwise
- **ssk:** slip, slip, knit slipped stitches tog. A decrease
- **st(s):** stitch(es)
- **tbl:** through back loop
- **ws or WS:** wrong side
- **yb:** yarn to the back
- **yfwd:** yarn forward

Index

Credits

Quintet would like to thank the following designers, who kindly supplied us with images for the book:

Tami Ely
www.DesignsbyTami.etsy.com
Skull and crossbones point protectors, page 8

Joan Miller
www.joanmiller.com
Glass cat bead, page 9

All other photographs and illustrations are the copyright of Quintet Publishing Ltd. While every effort has been made to credit contributors, Quintet would like to apologize should there have been any omissions or errors – and would be pleased to make the appropriate correction for future editions. Names, characters, businesses, places, events and incidents are either the products of the author's imagination or used in a fictitious manner. Any resemblance to actual persons, living or dead, or actual events is purely coincidental.

Author's Acknowledgements

Thanks to my mum for teaching me to knit, and to my dad for teaching me to appreciate a decent movie. Thanks to all at Quintet who have worked so hard to make this book happen. Thanks to my boys Frank and Henry for timing their arrivals just right, and most of all thanks to Matty Lewis, without whom this book could never have been written. Oh, and a tip of the hat to George Romero.

EVIL KNITS